Advance Praise for

Every Child Has a Thinking Style

"Since homework is now being assigned as early as kindergarten, learning organization skills has become more of an issue for students. This book is an important tool that can help parents help their children be successful in life as well as school."
—Jim Rogers
Executive Director, Sylvan Learning Center
Santa Rosa, California

"It is every early-childhood educator's dream to meet each individual need of each child in every class. Lanna Nakone's latest book, *Every Child Has a Thinking Style*, takes a giant leap in making this possible. As someone who has worked in programs for young children for thirty years, I'm thrilled to find a book that offers concrete solutions to the awesome challenge of bringing out the best in each child on the exciting road to adulthood. Lanna's newest book is a must-read for teachers."
—Judy Waggoner
Director, Concord Child Care Center, and
Chairperson, Contra Costa County Coalition of
Early Childhood Educators

"The parents in my parent-education program have benefited from Lanna's presentations. Many are frustrated by the demands placed on them and on their children, and by their children's apparent lack of ability to get organized. This book fills an important gap in children's developmental curriculum and is a valuable resource for parents and teachers."
—Jeff Kresge
Director St. Helena Co-Op
Nursery Director and Teacher,
Redwood Middle School

Praise for *Organizing for Your Brain Type*

"Lanna teaches you a life skill with an understandable approach to how you think and how you can get organized."

—Barry J. Izsak,
President, National Association of
Professional Organizers

"This very clever (and well-organized!) how-to helps you to identify your personality type, and then gives you easy step-by-step solutions for getting, and staying, organized. It is instructional and revealing."

—Lillian Vernon,
Founder, Lillian Vernon Corporation

"Organizing can be a primordial, gut-wrenching and finally a freeing experience. Read the book and find out for yourself how you and your family can take individualized approaches to get and stay organized."

—Margret McBride,
coauthor of *The One-Minute
Apology*, with Ken Blanchard

"Perfect for us artistic, passionate, nonconformist types. If your desk or home is a mess, get this book. Lanna's fun quiz nails how we function. Her solutions fit perfectly. Problem solved!"

—Susan Scott,
author of *Fierce Conversations:
Achieving Success at Work and in Life,
One Conversation at a Time*

Every Child Has a Thinking Style

A Guide to **Recognizing** and **Fostering** Each Child's Natural Gifts and Preferences—To Help Them Learn, Thrive, and Achieve

Lanna Nakone

THE BERKLEY PUBLISHING GROUP
Published by the Penguin Group
Penguin Group (USA) Inc.
375 Hudson Street, New York, New York 10014, USA
Penguin Group (Canada), 90 Eglinton Avenue East, Suite 700, Toronto, Ontario M4P 2Y3, Canada
(a division of Pearson Penguin Canada Inc.)
Penguin Books Ltd., 80 Strand, London WC2R 0RL, England
Penguin Group Ireland, 25 St. Stephen's Green, Dublin 2, Ireland (a division of Penguin Books Ltd.)
Penguin Group (Australia), 250 Camberwell Road, Camberwell, Victoria 3124, Australia
(a division of Pearson Australia Group Pty. Ltd.)
Penguin Books India Pvt. Ltd., 11 Community Centre, Panchsheel Park, New Delhi—110 017, India
Penguin Group (NZ), cnr. Airborne and Rosedale Roads, Albany, Auckland 1310, New Zealand
(a division of Pearson New Zealand Ltd.)
Penguin Books (South Africa) (Pty.) Ltd., 24 Sturdee Avenue, Rosebank, Johannesburg 2196,
South Africa

Penguin Books Ltd., Registered Offices: 80 Strand, London WC2R 0RL, England

Every effort has been made to ensure that the information contained in this book is complete and accurate. However, neither the publisher nor the author is engaged in rendering professional advice or ser-
vices to the individual reader. The ideas, procedures, and suggestions contained in this book are not
intended as a substitute for consulting with your physician. All matters regarding your health require
medical supervision. Neither the author nor the publisher shall be liable or responsible for any loss or
damage allegedly arising from any information or suggestion in this book.

PRINTING HISTORY
Perigee trade paperback edition / April 2006

ISBN: 0-399-53246-3

PERIGEE is a registered trademark of Penguin Group (USA) Inc.
The "P" design is a trademark belonging to Penguin Group (USA) Inc.

This book has been cataloged by the Library of Congress

PRINTED IN THE UNITED STATES OF AMERICA

10 9 8 7 6 5 4 3 2 1

Most Perigee Books are available at special quantity discounts for bulk purchases for sales promo-
tions, premiums, fund-raising, or educational use. Special books, or book excerpts, can also be created
to fit specific needs.

For details, write: Special Markets, The Berkley Publishing Group, 375 Hudson Street, New York,
New York 10014.

A child, too, can never grasp the face that the same mother who cooks so well, is so concerned about his cough, and helps so kindly with his homework, in some circumstances has no more feeling than a wall for his hidden inner world.

— Alice Miller, The Drama of the Gifted Child

To my brother Ward —
one of the first people who really "got me"
and became my lifelong intellectual buddy.
Where would I be without you?

Also, to Lucas Whittlesy Rostan —
my literary agent's baby son and my muse.
Without the creation of you,
there would be no book.
You little cutie!

CONTENTS

ACKNOWLEDGMENTS

My first book, *Organizing for Your Brain Type,* was just arriving in bookstores around the country when I showed up at the National Association of Professional Organizers (N.A.P.O.) conference in San Diego. I led a workshop called "Corporate Organizing: How to Get In!" and was honored to speak to a huge audience of more than four hundred organizers. It was a pivotal moment for me. I realized how so many giving, talented, and gutsy professional organizers were instrumental in helping me in the early years of my career in Los Angeles. I want to acknowledge N.A.P.O. founding members Ann Gambrell and Beverly Clower, who guided me to launch my business in 1999. Members of N.A.P.O.–Los Angeles Jean Furuya, Debbie Gilster, Dolores Kaytes, Christine Palen, and Karen Simon were very kind and shared so much inside knowledge to put me in the right direction. Other professional organizers who really motivated me are Sandra Ateca, Shawn Kershaw, Marianna Long, Judith Kolberg, Annie Rohrbach, Lisa Sarasohn, Valentina Sgro, Toni Scharff, Glorya Schklair, Sandy Stelter, Judy Stern, and Angela Wallace. Thank you all for your friendship and inspiration.

When it comes to getting a book published, my agent, Stephanie Kip Rostan, knows how to get the job done so well. She has become such a confidant, coach, and trustworthy ally. I'm blessed to have someone so knowledgeable about this business at my side to guide me in all my future writing possibilities. Also, I want to acknowledge my *fabulous* editor, Marian Lizzi, who bubbles with such passion, humor, and support that any writer can meet the deadline . . . well, almost! Thanks to all the talented people at Perigee Books who made this book really work, especially the graphic artist and designer, Liz Sheehan, who created those amazing animals. Just super! I wanted to express gratitude to all the writers in the bibliography but especially to such brilliant writers such as Steven Mintz, Ph.D., author of *Huck's Raft: The History of American Childhood*, which opened my heart; Dr. Dan Kindlon, Ph.D., author of *Too Much of a Good Thing*, which confirmed my suspicions of child rearing; and Dr. Hallowell, whose books *The Childhood Roots of Adult Happiness* and *A Walk in the Rain with a Brain* provides such tender, fun and peaceful solutions to our world.

This book would not have been written if it weren't for three important people in my life: Arlene Taylor, Ph.D., who provided me with an incredible methodology that has the possibility to changes people's lives, offered many insights and comments along the way, and is incredibly supportive of my work; Ilene Segalove, who gave me support, was willing to continuously bounce ideas back and forth, and who believes that my work is much more than traditional organizing and lifestyle choices, but rather it is about changing the world! (Hence my company: Organized World®=Peaceful World); and Jenny Kane, who wins the best girlfriend in the whole wide world award for the seventh year in a row! A big loving thank-you to my parents, Harry and Ann, for never withholding their love and always providing me with continual support and appreciation for all I've done. How blessed am I?

I would also like to thank some people who I forgot to thank in my first book (forgive me) or just mention them again because they are so darn special. My inspiring and yes, demanding professors at the University of Saskatchewan, Dr. Dayton, Dr. Farmer, Dr. Mullens, Dr. Swan, and Dr. Thompson. Thank you for giving me the opportunity to be heard and inspiring me to be just as intelligent as you! The one and only, Rev. Janet Garvey-Stangvik, Elsa Alonso and family, Patti Bloomfield, Dean and Rhonda Bowen, Stephanie Chu, Copperfields bookstore in Napa and Calistoga, Mary Edano, Angela Hoxsey, Gary and Pam Jaffe, Malka Johanson, Peggy Liles, Lea Ann and Bill McClendon, The Napa Valley Center for Spiritual Living, Net-Flow, NBOC (North Bay Organizers and Coaches), Sasha Paulsen at the *Napa Valley Register,* Ann Reilly, Vina Saycocie, Judy Waggoner, Smitty Wermuth, and Larry Hlavsa and the staff, especially Leslie Stanton in the children's corner at the St. Helena Library—a library that is ranked fourth out of 197 libraries in California, might I add.

I would also like to thank all the nursery schools to the high schools in Napa County, especially teachers like Leigh Paris, Christopher Melville, Sue Morgan, and Scott Dunyan, the headmaster at the Blue Oak School in Napa, who have all shared with me so much of their hands-on teaching experience. Last, but not least, a huge hug and gratitude to all of my young clients, the amazing children I've met over the years who have brought so much insight, passion, and humor into what I do. I thank you so very much. Your willingness to get organized (well kind of, "Mom, do we have to?") and seeing your rooms, grades, and life transform make me so happy. You deserve a life that is easy to maintain where all your gifts and talents can blossom.

—Lanna Nakone, summer 2005

FOREWORD BY

Arlene Taylor, Ph.D.

The program director and I looked through the one-way glass window. Dr. B, as everyone called her, had invited me to present a lecture on brain function for parents and teachers. In turn, I had asked permission to observe operations ahead of time. "It is an education in itself, just watching these preschoolers," she enthused. "Each one is so different!"

"That's because each brain is different," I agreed. "As different as the owner's thumbprint."

"Take Jerry for instance," Dr. B said as she gestured toward a little towhead. "He needs a place for everything and wants everything in its place. We assigned a portion of one of the cupboard shelves for his exclusive use."

"There goes Sally with her velvet patchwork bag." I watched a little girl in a bright red dress dump out the contents. Carefully she placed a teddy bear, a picture of her dog, a hair ribbon, a few seashells, and a box of crayons on the table. When everything was arranged to her satisfaction, she sat down at the table, opened her coloring book, and began to color. Dr. B chuckled and drew my attention to a little girl in a denim pantsuit who was writing something on a flip chart. "Ellie is as different from Sally as night is from day," she explained. "Ellie typically brings just a tablet and a marker to school. In fact, she has asked her parents for a laptop so she can go paperless!"

Dr. B pointed toward a tiny redheaded chap who was gazing

out the window. "When Sam sits still and looks out the window," she explained, "I know his little brain is processing at top speed. He comes up with the most unusual ideas—some of which are actually doable!" We chuckled. "And the boy with the ponytail. That's Kendall," Dr. B said. "He prefers to spend his free time curled up in the corner beanbag. My guess is that he's an extreme introvert." I nodded. "The teachers make sure there are a variety of books for him to read," she explained. "They affirm him when he participates and let him be the rest of the time."

We chatted about brain function as we observed the children in their preschool environment. "My goal," she explained, "is to give the children learning opportunities to build skills in all four divisions of the cerebrum while at the same time help them start identifying what their brains do easily. I want them to continue completing the blueprint already in their brain, to become the person each was designed to be."

What an unusual woman, I mused. She is applying brain-function information in a practical manner. No wonder parents sign up years in advance to reserve a place for their child. If you have to use daycare, this appears to be the bee's knees. What a difference her approach could make in the lives of these children!

Many parents, teachers, and care providers are not that savvy, although brain research is burgeoning in this twenty-first century. Researched conclusions from state-of-the-art brain scans (e.g., PET Scans, MRI, fMRI, SPECT), in combination with information available through other modalities, have led to the emergence of a new branch of science: *brain function.*

There are many ways to describe the brain. The cerebrum or gray matter is divided naturally into four divisions. Each division is believed to contain specific brain functions that help human beings develop specific types of skills, although there may be some overlap because the brain is so complex. Most human beings are believed to possess an innate brain advantage for processing information in one of the four divisions. (Biochemically, there is a reduced resistance to the transmission of information across the synaptic gap.) This unique advantage is energy efficient and impacts everything the person does for his or her entire life.

By the age of two, if children have been exposed to a variety of activities and have been encouraged to be who they were designed to be, their own brain advantage should begin to be evident, at least to some degree. The old axiom, *train children in the way they should go and when they are old they'll never depart from it,* makes incredible sense when viewed from this perspective. When the majority of your activities match what your brain does easily, and you are expending a fraction of the energy that is required as compared to utilizing functions from the other three divisions, why would you ever want to live another way?

Not long ago I heard a researcher say that most people have it backward in terms of brain function and long-term health and success. Many grew up believing that if you didn't have to work really hard at something, it wasn't worth anything. In actuality, if you identify a task or activity that is *easy* for your brain to accomplish (and yes, you'll still have to develop skills through practice), the activity is likely a good match with your brain's own advantage.

This brain advantage is so powerful that if you devote time, energy, and resources to honing skills that match what your brain does easily, you can attain a high level of competence, perhaps even outstanding. On the other hand, devote the same amount of time, energy, and resources into honing skills that are very energy-intensive for your brain, and mediocre performance may be about the best you can do. And in the process, you'll risk decreasing your health, happiness, overall success in life, and perhaps even longevity.

When children can be helped early in life to recognize what their brains do easily, they have just been handed one of the most valuable insurance policies that exists on this planet—and it didn't require years of monthly payments. It just took awareness, understanding, and a commitment to practically apply brain-function strategies on a daily basis.

Lanna Nakone, a professional organizer, has dedicated her work life to help adults manage their environments in ways that match what their brains do easily (refer to *Organizing for Your Brain Type,* published by St. Martin's Press) so they can maintain their environments with minimal energy expenditures. Brain-function research admonishes: focus on your strengths. Avoid, hire out, trade for, or collaborate on activities that are energy exhausting for your brain.

In this second book, Lanna has expanded this concept to assist parents, teachers, and care providers in managing their children's environments more effectively. I am 100 percent behind her efforts. After all, what is most important in the final analysis? Forcing children to expend great amounts of energy trying to maintain their environments in a way that is exhausting for their brains, or honing a relationship with them in an environment that is a good match for what their brains do easily? Both are unique, the child and the environment.

Use the information in this book to jump-start your viewing differences in a new light. Use it to reduce your frustration and help you give up unrealistic expectations. Use it to identify strategies that work in the long term for all the brains that need to interact in a given environment (at least at some level). Not only can it be fun, just think of the gift you are giving to the next generation!

Arlene Taylor, Ph.D.
brain-function specialist
www.arlenetaylor.org

CHAPTER 1

There's More Than One Way to Be Organized

Family life for many has become too much
work and too little fun.
—Dr. Robert Shaw, *The Epidemic*

When I was a child, my mother was just like Carol Brady from TV's *The Brady Bunch*. Order was her middle name. No joke, our living room resembled the perfect hotel lobby. Mom took pride knowing where each and every little thing went, and so, when I'd zip home from school searching for my jump rope, she would try to calm me down. "Lanna, remember dear, equipment for outside activities is stored in the garage, on the bottom left-hand shelf." Mom was the epitome of the ultimate organizer, whose motto comes as no surprise: "There is a place for everything and everything in its place."

My dad, on the other hand, was no shining star in the organizational department. He had many more important things to do, like shovel snow and tinker away in the garage. His desk was nearly invisible, piled a mile high with thousands of pieces of paper and articles on the latest in financial investing. Always in search of his car keys, Dad believed all things had legs because his stuff would inevitably walk away and hide, until Mom showed up, as usual, to save the day. As I grew older, I tried to fit into Mom's finely tuned system, but even when I tossed my winter boots into the official shoe cubby, it was never quite right. Mom wanted them lined up toe to toe, like in a Bloomingdales' display! Let's face it, when it came to organizing, Mom, Dad, and I were all very different. The solutions we desired and required were not the same. Why? Not because one of us was "right" or "wrong," but because each of us expressed our own innate organizing styles.

Like so many parents, my mother took our organizing differences personally and made it perfectly clear it was her way or the highway. She was housewife *extraordinaire.* However, because I was the child, I was labeled a tad "out of order" and had to try to mimic her way early on, or else. But was I really "out of order"? No, I was simply different from her. In the arcane world of organizing, if you aren't a stickler for neat as a pin, you are often considered inadequate. Organizing has been a rigid arena, and there haven't been many inclusive definitions that embrace our own unique styles—that is, until now! I believe all children need to be validated and honored, not cramped or molded to match their primary caregiver's organizing style. Homes must be organized to reflect the needs of all involved, and differences must be celebrated, not looked down upon or even attacked.

Many times I have come home after a full day of organizing a client and said to myself, "If my clients would have learned some basic organizing skills when they were young, they may not have needed me so desperately today." Yes, I bet their lives would have been much easier and they would have grown up with much more confidence, if only . . . This kind of thinking led me to the creation of a practical model that focuses on the particular needs and abilities of children, one that reflects their unique passions, skills, and identity.

Let's face it: it is exhausting to be a child these days. Children of all ages are faced with enormous expectations from family, friends, and society. They seldom have a moment to themselves, much less help to figure out what their strengths and weaknesses are. Five percent of American children suffer from depression, six million are now on Ritalin, and the number taking prescription psychiatric drugs has more than doubled in the last ten years. *They need our help now!* Is there something we can do in the organizing field to make life simpler, more functional, and more fulfilling so we need to medicate fewer kids? With commitment and shared vision from informed parents and teachers, we can create environments that really support a child's uniqueness and ability to handle their world in a way that builds confidence and well-being. A little time invested right now to learn more about how your child thinks and what his or her brain style is can and will pay back enormous dividends in the future.

But how do we go about organizing so everyone's needs are met without feeling personally attacked or invalidated? The answer is both profound and simple. We must wake up to the fact that there is more than one approach to getting kids organized! I know, firsthand, how difficult and frustrating it is to march to a different drumbeat, and so I was inspired and mobilized to address the special needs, abilities, and styles of each and every child with my book on organizing geared specifically to kids. How ultimately liberating for the child and the parent or teacher.

I passionately believe the job of parents, teachers, caregivers, nannies, and anyone who has children is to understand what works for a child, how they learn, and what comes naturally to them. Working hands-on, in the organizing trenches, with so many children and families over the years, I have witnessed children fail time and time again as organizing systems were put into place and didn't resonate with what the child does easily and effortlessly. If we can identify what comes easily to them, the next obvious step is to build skills that support him or her to be their best self. As Alice Miller states in the classic, *The Drama of the Gifted Child,* "If a child is lucky enough to grow up with a mother who allows herself to be made use of as a function of the child's development—then a healthy self-feeling can gradually develop in the growing child." We all want to make our children's lives easier and more fulfilling, not more difficult for them in placing organizing systems that don't ultimately really work for them.

Being a Kid Isn't What It Used to Be

> Kids who have more materialistic values are unhappier, distressed, and engage in risky behavior.
>
> —Juliet B. Schor, *Born to Buy*

The urgency to get organized and to create a consciousness about it with children must be addressed. Over the last couple of years, I've spent a good deal of time organizing in hundreds of family homes. At least half of my residential organizing business is geared to creating systems for children. Just last week, I spent more than ten hours organizing a fifth grader's room in Berkeley. (Ironically, her mother's doctor's office took less than that the week before.) In this process, I have noticed the stuff of life growing by the mile. I cannot believe the huge volume of children's toys (I call them "toy cemeteries") piling up in living rooms and dens; the weight of school backpacks, so heavy that they resemble check-in baggage storage for airplanes; not to mention the grueling and complex morning productions (from feeding to grooming) to get the kids out the door by 8 A.M. *Way too much work,* I've thought to myself, *There must be a better way.* Everyone is working much of the time, and still no one ever feels that they are getting ahead. As one mother once said to me, "Why am I always organizing their rooms but feel that they are never that organized? Why bother?" "Too much to do and too little time," is what I always hear from parents. Parents feel that they have to "jumpstart" their child every day, even if it means sacrificing their own needs time and time again.

As Kathy Hirsh-Pasek, the author of *Einstein Never Used Flash Cards,* reminds us, we are now "in the cult of achievement and the loss of childhood." The following statistics shed some light on the life of a typical child today. The picture shows a pretty extreme polarity of children who are overindulged, almost drowning in the busyness of excessive activities and consuming goods, and the children who are alone and who are without role models and active support. I've noticed over the years that many parents tend to be either overbearing and controlling or too hands-off and passive, seldom taking the time to really converse with their children about basic skills, observe the outcomes, and create modifying solutions.

- Children from the age of 4-12 have tripled their purchases since the 1990s.

Howe, Neil. *Millennials Rising.* New York: Vintage Books, 2000.

- Children's homes have 50% more things in them since the 1980s. **Howe, Neil. *Millennials Rising*. New York: Vintage Books, 2000.**

- Since the 1920s toys have been marketed directly to children. **Mintz, Steven. *Huck's Raft*. Cambridge: Harvard University Press, 2004.**

- Roughly 2.4 million children from the ages of 5-13 are responsible for themselves after school. **Newberger, Eli. *The Men They Will Become*. Cambridge: Perseus Publishing, 1999.**

- In 2004, 15 billion dollars were spent on advertising to children. **Schor, Juliet. *Born to Buy*. New York: Scribner, 2004.**

- 80% of global branding is focused on the tweeny category, from the first to the sixth grade. **Schor, Juliet. *Born To Buy*. New York: Scribner, 2004.**

- There are over 150,000 toys on the market. **Declements, Barthe. *Spoiled Rotten*. New York: Hyperion Books, 1996.**

- In 1975, 34% of mothers with children under the age of six worked outside the home. **Hirsh-Pasek, Kathy. *Einstein Never Used Flashcards*. New York: St. Martin's Press, 2003.**

- In 1999, 61% of mothers with children under the age of six worked outside the home. **Hirsh-Pasek, Kathy. *Einstein Never Used Flashcards*. New York: St. Martin's Press, 2003.**

- In 1997, The International Labor Organization claimed that fathers were working 51 hours per week and mothers were working 41 hours per week.

Hirsh-Pasek, Kathy. *Einstein Never Used Flashcards.* **New York: St. Martin's Press, 2003.**

- In the 1940's 80% of kids grew up with both parents. In the 1990s there is less than a 50% chance of growing up with both parents. **Covey, Stephen.** *The 7 Habits of Highly Effective Families.* **New York: Golden Books, 1997.**

- In 1981, kids had 40% time for play. In 1997, kids have 25% of time for play. **Hirsh-Pasek, Kathy.** *Einstein Never Used Flashcards.* **New York: St. Martin's Press, 2003.**

- Children have a third less downtime than they did a generation ago. **Kindlon, Dan.** *Too Much of a Good Thing.* **New York: Hyperion, 2001.**

- Since 1981, homework for children 12 and under has increased 50%. **Kindlon, Dan.** *Too Much of a Good Thing.* **New York: Hyperion, 2001.**

- 75% of children's self-talk is negative. **Isaccs, Susan and Wendy Ritchey.** *I Think I Can I Know I Can.* **New York: St. Martin's Press, 1989.**

- White-collar families provide twice as much positive feedback as working-class parents and five times more than parents who are on welfare. **Bellamy, Rufus.** *Inside the Brain.* **North Mankato, MN: Smart Apple Media, 2005.**

No wonder kids are so disorganized and parents are so stressed out. Their environments have become extremely difficult, complex, and ultimately hard to manage. The more parents buy, the more children want, and the more children want, the tendencies to get more disorganized rise as parents have less time to teach and follow through.

In the 1960s and 1970s, middle-class parents wanted their children to have everything they didn't have growing up. They opted for less discipline and thought that the best way to show how much you loved your children was to give them everything they wanted and do everything for them. Being your child's butler or spa attendant isn't doing anyone any good in the long run. Ironically, saying no to their myriad daily wants and not buying them everything shows more love and concern rather than less. Their toy cemetery doesn't bring families together, but rather it requires a great deal of upkeep. If the little time you have with your child is about purging and rearranging just their Barbie stuff and Kelli dolls, it can be enough to ruin a family night! Chances are that the more TV they watch, the more they want and, therefore, organizing must begin at the store, not just after the stuff is home. After you buy it, the stuff needs to be organized—and who has the time or the desire to do it?

Some days when I organize a child's room, I don't know if I've landed at Toys R Us or a bookstore. Their bedrooms, which should be a place for sleeping, are now storage facilities—filled with everything their little hearts desire. As one of my clients' daughter said recently, "Why are we always purging Mommy, when you are the one buying me things?" Although we may not want to admit it, more likely than not, we have created self-indulgent kids who, on one hand, have no meaningful consequences for actions, or on the other hand, are being asked to do way too much. Recently, I was working in a home where the eight-year-old son was asked to do the evening dishes by himself, because "Mommy needs to return a couple e-mails."

When the environment gets really out of hand, parents and child educators need to avoid being myopic. They need to step back and be more interested in their child's development, responsibility, and full potential, not just getting another chore done! As Dan Kindlon, a Harvard psychology professor, points out, "We undermine their character development . . . by covering up issues with money; we deprive them of the opportunity to earn important coping skills, a realistic sense of their strengths and limitations."

Nowadays, kids need to understand that organizing their world, in their own style, is a vital way to set off on a road to success. When I went to Holliston Elementary School and Aden Bowen Collegiate for my high school, I don't ever remember taking a class in organization or time management. However, in schools across North America today, teachers are teaching their students the value of being organized. In a fourth-grade class in southern California, a teacher has carved out the first ten minutes and the last ten minutes of the day as "agenda and binder organize" and has designated Fridays, "clean out your backpack day."

Finally, as caregivers, you are about to be made conscientious about organizing and be supported on all fronts on the value of this extraordinary skill: how to plan your child's life, organize his or her time, juggle a variety of different tasks, and eventually be a team player at home and at school. You are teaching your child valuable skills and helping them know that they are an important part of your family and valued in the community.

Organizing Is a Parenting Skill

In Latin, the word *discipline* means "teaching" or "learning." Traditional organizing attempts fail because we demand rather than teach or explain how to do things. Parents and educators often fail to keep in mind a child's physical and intellectual development when instructing them to be better organized. As Stephen Covey says organization is, "creating order and systems to help accomplish what is valued by the family." Eventually, children will be organized to what works for them and have more pressure-free time when they can chill out and relax.

Every one of us is dealing with an overload of busyness, information assault, and pressure. I'm in the organizing trenches every day, and I see the results of an overly busy, uncertain, and highly pressured life for families. *Every Child Has a Thinking Style* will put some peace back into your life and give you the quality of life you deserve, with less stress and mess, while helping you feel more confident and successful as a parent. This book is a confidence-builder for all involved! More importantly, it will make someone who is very special in your life happier and help him or her go through life with fewer bumps.

That is what this book is really all about—deepening your appreciation and understanding of your child's innate giftedness, while offering real tools to help you maximize and better cope with all aspects of their ever-growing lives. If their environment for learning is the same as their environment where they are happiest, feel most comfortable, and are organized to fit "their" style, then you are on the right path. Organizing isn't about putting their art from school in a box labeled "Memorabilia—Grade 4." Rather, it is about organizing with a capital "O," where you are creating an environment in which they feel comfortable in, are most productive, and, therefore, are the happiest. You are building on their natural interest and desires and supporting and encouraging who they truly are. As Maria Montessori, one of the first doctors and educators to apply science to an understanding of children's behavior in the classroom, states, "Order is one of the needs of life, which, when it is satisfied, produces a real happiness . . . it is one of the most pleasant and spontaneous tasks they perform."

Children Want to Be Organized—Get Them Started!

> The biggest suggestions I could use about organizing my children would be to have greater patience and understanding about their interpretation or organization. I believe children have different ways of organizing, and sometimes it is hard to accept different, especially when they're your own.
>
> —Denise Eyre, *mother of two and teacher*

Maria Montessori said that "The first thing a child's education demands is the provision of an environment in which they can develop the powers given to them by nature." Montessori argued that children have a basic need for organization; she called it creating a "prepared" space. She emphasized that this space takes precedence over *all* other social needs. She also believed that in the right kind of environment, a child would express him- or herself on a much higher level, with more enthusiasm and focus, than in a space that did not honor personal needs. I couldn't agree with her more. Children desperately want to create order out of confusion, each in his or her own way.

This book presents an effective organizing system for children from the ages of seven to thirteen, to support and inspire them in primary school up until they graduate middle school. Rudolph Steiner called these years the "heart of childhood," as they are run more by a feeling for life than thinking about life, and their brains are still, as one neurologist claims, "a work in progress." At seven or eight, children already are becoming conscious of right and wrong. They are now able to stand on their own feet and are building independence, by wanting to help and mimic their caregivers, but they are still trainable. They understand responsibility, cause and effect, and consequences, and they are able to make sense of their surroundings.

By the ninth or tenth year, with minimal help from the parent, children are capable and extremely independent. At this age, they can operate every electrical appliance in the home, from the DVD player to the dishwasher. Kids are finally at an age where they can take care of their things and themselves, yet still respect parents and are willing to take direction. It's the perfect time to teach them how to organize in their own unique way. As Eleanor Reynolds, the author of *Guiding Young Children,* claims, "The environment in which children spend their days does directly influence their thoughts, feelings, behavior, health, creativity and relationships. Thus, helping them at this early age of planning their environment will greatly enhance their quality of life."

Rather than making it another power struggle, this book helps you make it fun, a game, an act of discovery. How much is your child able to fully express him- or herself? How much more joy can be in his or her life? Helping your child become more self-sufficient at this age can make the rest of his or her life less hectic and more fulfilling. To train your child well, in a way that ensures they respect themself, will make them fly and give them the self-assurance and validation they need to become a success-ful and contributing human being in the world.

At this age, many significant things are happening in a child's life—and in the brain itself. Brain researchers find that the prefrontal cortex undergoes phenomenal change. As authors Marian Diamond and Janet Hopson describe in their book *Magic Trees of the Mind,* "if the brain is stimulated, dendritic branching and growth continue throughout the child's middle years. . . . At the same time, though, excess synaptic connections are more and more heavily weeded." As a result, your child's brain keeps what it needs and discards what it doesn't, and this allows the brain to think more effectively and efficiently. Or, as the authors of *The Scientist in the Crib* put it, "the brain seems better than most of us at getting rid of unused clutter. It throws out the things that don't work and keeps the things that do." Just think, you are so-lidifying the organizing skills in your child's genetic makeup by being concerned and conscientious about how he or she is getting organized.

Simultaneously, their young brains have such an excess of synapses that pruning is a really healthy process. As Dr. Deborah Yurgelun-Todd, a neuron-psychologist, claims, "Good judgment is learned, but you can't learn it if you don't have the necessary hardware." This is the time of your child's life when he or she is building and really organizing how the brain develops, and your contribution right now will ensure better, more efficient connec-tions, fundamentally creating a healthier road map for your child to deal with the rest of his or her life! A little investment now may go a very long way in the future of how your child lives their life. Making life easier for all involved is what I'm after!

What a gift! As we learn how to make our children and others conscientious of their own organizing style at this early age, chances are when they hit late adolescence and beyond, they will be more prone to have a style that is comfortable for them and in turn, will allow them to communicate with you more easily, never mind having an edge as they adjust to the ever-changing variables in school and their personal world. Catching them at this appropriate age category from seven to fourteen and planting and reaffirming their organizing preferences can make children feel more confident and self-accepting before the fears and worries of the adolescenct years set in.

Can you imagine your child having a well-developed and practiced organizing style when they reach college? So start A.S.A.P. Help them build stronger and better connections in their brain so basic skills are already in place for the trying teenage years. Remember that their neural circuitry, or hardware, takes years to get up and running, until the early twenties, or longer, so be patient. Perhaps you picked up this book and your children are already in their teenage years. Don't worry; you still can make an impact. It is never too late, just a tad harder putting a behavior into place. You will be at least able to understand why they do the things they do and approach behavior modification in a language that works for them.

Organic Organization

In my first book, ***Organizing for Your Brain Type,*** I defined "being organized" as the ability to find something in five minutes or less in an environment based on what I call "organic structure."

Organic is the word I use to define people discovering their own organizing solutions based on their own innate styles of doing and being. "Organic" organizing feels like second nature because when it's organic, it reflects each person's talents. This results in a feeling of ease—instead of fight or flight—when confronting the task of putting things away or making them available. The one surefire way to find success is to use a system that is an extension of who you really are, something that makes sense, is easy to do, and doesn't zap your energy. Everyone's organizing style comes from within. As Michelangelo once said, "Inside every stone or marble dwells a beautiful statue. One needs only to remove excess material to reveal the work of art within." *Every Child Has a Thinking Style* provides you with the chisel and the mallet to discover what is already there.

Children also love to help. Yes, they need guidance, and it is your job to set an example, but they want to pitch in, work alongside, and please you. Children tend to bring a playful exuberance when solving any challenge they face. Everyone wants happy, healthy lives for their children, but they don't always know the best way to go about it. If you spend the time to digest and apply these ideas, you and your child will make strides toward the relationship you've always wanted, with sanity and calmness for you and joy and safety for your child. Also, imagine the time you'll save when you no longer have to harp and rail and tire yourself out saying things that go in one ear and out the other. You'll be able to spend that time on real issues that concern you and your children, instead—or at least have more fun!

"Where do I sign up?" you ask? Look no further. Finally, an approach that takes different needs and strategies to the realm of organization, where everyone fits into a thinking style and no one is valued less for thinking a certain way. They all are important, and need to be celebrated. As the prophet Khalil Gibran said, "You are the bows from which your children as living arrows are sent forth." Now, let's understand how you can aim that bow in the right direction!

Your Brain Knows

> The news is that children's brains are much busier than ours. At birth each neuron in the cerebral cortex has around 2,500 synapses. The number of synapses reaches its peak at two or three years of age, when there are about 15,000 synapses per neuron. This is actually many more than in an adult brain . . . from the point of view of neurology they really are alien geniuses. By three months old the infant brain areas involved in seeing, hearing and touch are consuming a huge amount of glucose. That means things are cooking! By three years old the child's brain is actually twice as active as an adult brain.
>
> —Alison Gopnik, Andrew N. Meltzoff, and Patrica K. Kuhl,
> *The Scientist in the Crib*

As you read in the preceding quote, scientists today around the globe are actively studying the complexities of the human brain.

With more than 400,000 Internet sites dedicated to brain research and education, valuable insights about how all of us learn are being discovered and discussed. Children are naturally an area of great interest, and the relationship between the brain and how children learn at home and in the classroom is being investigated as scientists actually watch a child's thinking in motion! Thank goodness for MRIs, PET scans, and other testing devices, because they allow us to draw some astonishing conclusions about the thinking brain. Computerized charts show electrical and chemical changes as children do math problems, play games, or put together puzzles. It is all simply amazing to see what the future of brain research has to discover.

In the past, professional organizers tended to take this information and impose the traditional "left-brain/right-brain" formula to define a particular individual's organizing traits: are they a left-brain organizer, that is, very analytical and logical about what they keep and how they use it, or are they a right-brain organizer, that is, very creative and fun about their space? But understanding how the brain operates is far more complicated than that! There are so many other ways of understanding thinking and doing, such as sequential and random, verbal and nonverbal, symbolic and concrete, logical and intuitive, temporal and nontemporal. Thank goodness there is so much insight into the living mind that we can seek much more accurate correlations among the complexities of thinking styles, brain development, and our children's behavior.

As a result of ongoing research, scientists tend to agree that there are basically four divisions of cerebral tissue, although there is still disagreement about how to label or identify them. I was fortunate enough to meet and work with Dr. Arlene Taylor, a brain function specialist, who introduced me to the work of Dr. Katherine Benziger, creator of the Benziger Thinking Styles Assessment. I applied brain-function research to the question of how the brain processes organization and combined this information with Dr. Benziger's model, which utilizes a series of questions to help determine which of the four quadrants (basal or frontal lobe/left or right hemisphere) of the brain a person tends to unmake easily. From this profound pool of information, I developed a sensible and workable solution that describes how the distinct quadrants of the brain motivate us to do, decide, act, and organize. Understanding what drives or inspires children is a great piece of knowledge in making their life more purposeful and, therefore, more peaceful.

Each of us has a brain quadrant that we prefer. It is the place we come from when we take in the world, process it, and affect it. When our style of expression, living, acting, and organizing comes from our preferred quadrant, we are operating from a place that energizes rather than depletes us. PET scans have demonstrated that our brains expend differing amounts of energy, depending on the type of task we are performing and whether or not it matches what our brain does easily. Because our preference for processing information is one of the four natural divisions of the cerebrum or thinking brain, it should come as no surprise that if there is a reduced resistance to the transmission of information between neurons (thinking cells), then we experience less stress and overall fatigue.

To be more specific, most mental functions are lateralized in the brain. In PET scan studies, the hemisphere that is in charge of a particular task (left or right/front or back) glowed more brightly when compared to the matching areas in the opposite hemisphere.

This can help identify which physical part of our brain (left front, left rear, right front, or right rear) dominates our thinking preferences. Most people are believed to have a quadrant preference. We're probably happier and healthier when 51 percent of our activities use our quadrant of preference. Of course, we all use all four quadrants at different times, but again, one is our most natural source of motivation and behavior, and this is true of your children's maturing brains as well.

Organizing for Their Brain Type
—The Only Way to Go!

> If we can recognize each child's thinking style and understand their strengths and weaknesses, we can sculpt a mind at a time.
> —Dr. Mel Levine, *A Mind at a Time*

Sue Person, the author of *I.T.I.: Integrated Thematic Instruction Teachers Manual,* writes, "Remember, form dictates function. Create an environment that helps shape [their] behavior." Basic routines generate more security, a less-stressed-out atmosphere, and an opportunity to figure out what really matters. Spending an extra five minutes and noticing what comes naturally to them and creating an organizing system that is easy for them to maintain must be set forth by the caregiver. Leading the way, setting an example, being authentic to you, and observing what is authentic to them is probably the most important thing on your parental to-do list. As Stephen H. Glenn and Jane Nelson, authors of *Raising Self-Reliant Children,* put it, "Pampering directly inhibits the development of self-discipline. Children learn only in an environment in which they have opportunities to identify themselves." Wow! What a concept in using contemporary brain-function research to help children make their lives a little less stressful and just plain easier.

However, *Every Child Has a Thinking Style* is actually much more than a new organizing system; it is a groundbreaking approach to understanding and supporting your child based on identifying his or her inherent talents and tendencies and then translating this personal profile into not just a set of practical organizing solutions, but how they approach school, play, activities, and living with others! Welcome to an all-encompassing way of focusing on their natural talents and tendencies and helping them build a life that reflects who they truly are. "If only you and your parents would have had a book like this when you were being raised" you say, but don't feel bad. Just think that you are seeing your child in a new way that probably hasn't been ever done before. In a layperson's terms, "Meyers-Briggs for kids"? Well, not exactly, but close!

My deep interest and concern for children lead to my decision to do serious research to educate myself and build the information necessary to translate my *Organizing for Your Brain Type* book to apply to parents and children. Not being an expert can be an advantage, as I'm looking for practical rather than theoretical and academic solutions to understand the reasons behind children's clutter and come up with ways to develop some skills before they become young adults and are on their own. As a professional organizer who has observed, interacted, and dealt hands-on with hundreds of children, both clients, close friends, and family members, I have the practical and theoretical advantage to make solutions work and have seen the results years later.

With a little thought, you are going to be able to set up a working system that supports your child's overall basic needs. This can help your child find comfort, safety, and confidence as he or she navigates in an ever-changing world. This takes time and patience, but the results are amazing! Together, you will be able to implement positive changes in the environment that really work. The kids will not only learn how to be responsible for their stuff, but have fun doing it in a way that reflects their unique personality. And for you, the parent or teacher, there are rewards galore: less work, less nagging, and much more time enjoying each other.

The Four Organizing Types

> Change the environment; do not try to change
> the man [woman].
>
> —Richard Buckminster Fuller, *Design Science*

Combining years of professional organizing in hundreds of settings with the application of contemporary brain research has helped me recognize four distinct organizing patterns. As a leader in the organizing profession and a former academic and accomplished businessperson, I have given birth to a concept, probably ten years ahead of traditional organizing methodology, that goes like this: how a child thinks, what his or her natural brain lead is, and how he or she goes about getting organized must be intertwined for a child to be successful. It is as simple as that. Working at schools and at learning centers, I have seen children forced into an organizing style that reflects the needs of a parent or a teacher, that is completely antithetical to who the children are. And the parent or teacher wonder why their child is so disorganized!

There are natural ways human beings innately organize their belongings and their worlds, some tailored specifically to the wants and needs of children. Some children want to do it themselves and finish everything they start; others may want to finish organizing their room, but connecting with people triumphs the emphasis over their environment; others have their heads in the clouds and are almost unaware of their environment unless they are told about it or they need something in it to support their ideas; and some children want to direct others to manage it for them.

These approaches provide effective solutions to clutter, but more importantly, they provide a feeling of safety, support, and well-being. Building self-esteem, confidence, and courage in the lives of children is what may be the result if children are able to get organized in a way that works for them. Because children don't have a lot of space to be themselves, creating an environment that reinforces their natural needs and abilities can make the day-to-day struggles a lot less overwhelming and create less conflict at home and in school by focusing more on the joy of living rather than the struggle of the mundane and the basic needs of every day.

By reading and practically applying the information in this book, you will soon come to understand your child's unique thinking style and even celebrate the fact that, although it may be different than yours, it works and supports your child. If you had four children with four different brain preferences, you may find yourself saying, "So that is why my son prefers doing his

homework on the kitchen table at the same time every day."
(Maintainer) Or, "So that is why she keeps every vacation
photo." (Harmonizer) Or, "So that is why my daughter is always
running late to her swimming lessons." (Innovator) Or, "So this
is why his desk at school has virtually nothing in it." (Prioritizer)

The four distinct kinds of organizing are: *Maintainer:* These
children come from the world of To Organize; they epitomize the
classic "a place for everything and everything in its place." *Harmonizer:* These children come from the world of To Personalize;
they have an emotional connection to their things and to what
they symbolize. *Innovator:* These children come from the world
of To Innovate; they are much more likely to stack their belongings and have things out in the open—if it's out of sight it's out of
mind. *Prioritizer:* These children come from the world of To Analyze; they like to be in control of their environment to make
quick decisions and prefer to delegate most organizing tasks. In
more detail:

Maintainers—Mascot: "The Penguin"

- The Penguin follows routines and is very predictable.
- Brain location: The basal (back) left hemisphere.
- This part of the brain helps us maintain systems and places an
  emphasis on existing routines.
- Children gifted in this area prefer a structured and "traditional"
  organizing environment.
- They are the natural masters of organization and need only be
  supported in what society rewards them for doing.

Harmonizers—Mascot: "The Dog"

- The Dog thrives in packs with other dogs, and so the Dog style loves human company. Dogs are known to bury bones and precious toys in the yard. By gathering toys and items of past experiences, Harmonizers tend to collect a great deal of stuff and have issues parting with it.
- Brain location: The basal (back) right hemisphere.
- This part of the brain helps us develop a sense of harmony and connectedness.
- Children gifted in this area desire organization if it enhances their relationships and helps them keep their environment peaceful.
- These children tend to focus on other people's needs first and their needs and things second.

Innovators—Mascot: "The Horse"

- The Horse is unpredictable and likes to be free and unstructured but also can be extremely focused in a particular situation and is the vehicle for covering wide distances both literally, in space, and imaginatively, in creative endeavors.
- Brain location: The frontal/right hemisphere.
- This part of the brain helps all of us envision possibilities, imagine, and also make real changes.
- Children gifted in this area have a unique "stacking" system for managing their environment and need to have things out, right in front of them, as much as possible.
- They tend to live by the axiom "out of sight, out of mind."

- Innovator children have a strong aversion to daily routines and repetitive maintenance tasks.
- They need easy, "maintenance-free" and fun organizing strategies—nothing else will work!

Prioritizers—Mascot: "The Lion"

- The Lion wants to be the master of its environment, and its agility enables them to be quick to the chase and hit the bull's-eye time and time again.
- Brain location: The frontal/left hemisphere.
- This is the part of the brain that helps us set and achieve goals.
- Children gifted in this area like order but prefer to delegate the tasks of organizing and maintaining to others.
- Prioritizing children tend to want to be in charge, give directions, and make decisions to delegate.
- If organizing structures are minimal but functional, the Prioritizer will flourish.

When you identify your child's authentic organizing style, you will get to know your child in a new and more intimate way. The good new is, you will no longer have to view their behavior—be it obsessing about everything being just so, crying over the loss of something seemingly insignificant, running late, or not picking up their clothes—as a personal affront. You are finally able to help them develop skills, not give them pills, and provide working strategies and options that make sense to them, not just to you.

As you will soon learn, traditional organizing, the "everything in its place" modality, is really only accomplished loosely by the Maintainer. That means, perhaps, only a quarter of the child population desires and is capable of maintaining their bedroom in a way that resembles the cover of the current *Real Simple* magazine. Certainly, you've seen the photos of perfect kids' rooms and said, "How did that happen?" It is certainly not the solution for everyone—nor should it be! The other 75 percent of children have very little desire to get organized in that traditional way, but they have their own inner drive, their inner purpose for keeping things in a way that corresponds to their purpose in life. Whether these three other brain preferences are about people, possibility, or about progress, finding out that basic need and approaching organizing from that perspective won't make it just bearable, but it may make the child's life more successful and the parent's life more enjoyable.

Other Pieces of the Organizing Puzzle

Many other modalities can help you understand the particulars of your child's personality. Looking at some of them can help shed even more light on your child's organizing strengths and organizing challenges. I will share with you more tools and skills that will assist you as you design a system that supports their thinking style. Taking a couple quick quizzes to figure out the sensory preference and where they are in the Extroversion/Introversion model, we will closely examine those areas as well as the area of Gender Differences. Having this extra knowledge about your child's preferences will not only solidify their organizing systems, but also will make the entire process more enjoyable and easier on them. It will also greatly assist you, the caregiver, in the way you approach this conversion and communicate to your child.

Your Child's Sensory Preference

> Studies have shown that most of us spend
> 80 percent of our waking hours communicating.
> We relate with others (communicate) through
> the sensory systems. The question becomes, *Is
> our communication as effective as possible?*
> —Arlene Taylor, *"The Brain Program Syllabus"*

We take information in from the outside world through our senses. How we absorb this abundance of data has a profound impact on everything we do, including how we organize! By the age of five or six, a child usually begins to develop one sense that registers in his or her brain more quickly than the others. Be it visual (sight through the eyes), auditory (sound through the ears), or kinesthetic (touch/through the skin, taste/through the mouth, smell/through the nose), one of those three will be his or her primary channel for filtering information. About 60 percent of the population has a visual preference, 20 percent has an auditory, and 20 percent has a kinesthetic preference. It is interesting to note that more boys tend to have a visual preference, while more girls tend to be auditory.

How does this work? Decoding centers for the sensory systems are housed in the six lobes of the thinking brain—three in the left and three in the right cerebral hemisphere. These are better known as the occipital lobes, temporal lobes, and parietal lobes. These lobes are able to receive and decode up to 10 million bits of data per second—far more than we are capable of processing at a conscious level of awareness. If you are aware of which type of sensory data or stimuli registers in your child's brain most quickly, you are able to create a world that is more available, engaging for them, and easier to maintain.

For example, if your child is visual, his food must look just right. This child is often extremely sensitive to things he sees in the environment, like shadows on the wall or even the color of his bedroom. He also learns most easily by seeing how something is done rather than reading about it. An auditory child is sensitive to how things sound. They may love the whir of the ceiling fan or find it terribly annoying. They learn most easily by listening to or reading directions on how something is done and often relax best to music. A kinesthetic child prefers toys that feel good to the touch (smooth or soft), food needs to be just the right temperature and not scratchy in their throat, and they learn most easily by actually doing things in a hands-on style. Each child's sensitivity is a pure expression of their being, and being sensitive, in turn, is a way to truly honor and love them.

Helping your child feel alive and validated by his or her surroundings is the mission here! You want your child to feel good about his or her home life, and you want to encourage them to find their own way and eventually become responsible individuals. When a child receives sensory data in his or her preferred sensory system, he or she is not only able to retain information for a longer period of time, but also have easier access to it for recall.

Extroverts and Introverts

> When I approach a child, he inspires in me two
> sentiments: tenderness for what he is, and
> respect for what he may become.
>
> —Louis Pasteur, *www.wisdomquotes.com*

Is your child an extrovert, ambivert, or an introvert? This is another classification that helps us discover more about who we are and how we relate to each other, our environment, and the world. By taking the short quiz that follows, you can see where your child fits on the scale. For our focus, I will discuss the extroverts and introverts, but not ambiverts, as they are the ones in the middle with a bit of both tendencies. For example, an extrovert tends to require significant amounts of stimulation. Introverts require significant relief from stimulation to feel comfortable and function well.

Where your child stands on this continuum has a lasting influence on how he or she will learn certain skills and techniques. When you are tuned in to whether your child is understimulated or overstimulated, you can make significant alterations to help them interact with their world optimally. For example, if your child tends to be more on the introverted side, it is best to give them some downtime when they come home from school before you ask them to pick up their belongings or start their homework. If your child tends to be more on the extroverted side, it is great to openly support their organizing and even be there to help them do it.

According to social scientists, approximately 15 percent of the population is extremely extroverted, and 15 percent are extremely introverted. Seventy percent of the population falls in between the extremes. When your child or student is in this middle range, their brain will function most efficiently with moderate amounts of stimulation. They may tolerate high levels of stimulation for short periods of time but then usually require some downtime for recovery.

Scientists believe infants as young as a few days old already show signs of a tendency toward being an introvert or an extrovert. For example, an infant with extreme needs for stimulation (extrovert) may require less sleep and may only stop crying when its caregivers hold and play with him or her. An infant with very low needs for stimulation (introvert) may sleep longer and only stop crying when placed in a quiet room. Infants who express a middle range have more equal needs for stimulation and relief from stimulation.

This concept can also be used to create a supportive environment for your child and is extremely helpful when you begin helping them get organized. When you know your child's tendencies, you can reduce or amplify incoming data and information to accommodate their needs. For example, Susan is an extrovert, and Peter an introvert. When they tackle a particular organizing project, Susan requires a significant amount of stimulation, such as music, noise, friends, or family in the same room with her. Peter requires significant relief from stimulation and does not want music, conversations, or people hanging around bothering him. Their environments will look different, too: Susan prefers a lot of stuff, colors, motion, or patterns; without it, she can become bored, restless, or even fall asleep. Peter, on the other hand, prefers to have very little going on in his bedroom. If there is too much stuff—too many colors, too much motion, or too many patterns—he may tend to become agitated, sick, or even depressed.

The Role of Gender

> The boy more naturally involved himself in
> experiences that sharpen spatial skills; the girl
> involved herself more in experiences that
> strengthen inter-personal skills.
>
> —Anne Moir and David Jessel, *Brain Sex*

Boys and girls exhibit certain inherent male and female biological/ nature characteristics as well as challenges. They tend to make different friendship choices, have different dating patterns, and follow different career paths. Boys and girls are also socialized, reared, and guided in different ways. Gender differences need to be recognized and understood, or they will surely become a source of conflict and misunderstanding. When it comes to organizing, this difference becomes quickly apparent.

In our culture, females are typically responsible for the day-to-day tasks of keeping a household running, and women often pick up after a male partner and children without thinking twice about it. Even if your daughter participates in many other tasks, there is a greater chance that she will be expected to take care of the tedious, detail-specific work. Because women tend to fall into the category of perfectionists more than men, wanting the environment and the things in it "just so," they often view these tasks as pleasant, or at least as a way to find fulfillment, comfort, and a sense of self-assurance and even peace.

In his latest book, *The Essential Difference: Men, Women and the Extreme Male Brain*, Simon Baron-Cohen discusses how male and female brains are of a slightly different structure. If men have more brain cells than women, women have more dendritic connections than men. Women have a larger corpus collusum, which means they have the ability to operate with more freedom between the brain's two hemispheres that enhance collaborations between the brain's halves. Girls tend to excel at long-range planning and global thinking, while males excel at short-term planning, lateralized thinking, and goal attainment.

The list of comparisons can go on and on. But one thing is for sure: when it comes to organizing, men tend to do it when it is scheduled in their day planner or preferably encouraged by someone else who may even act as an assistant. Many girls have an emotional need to keep things, whereas some boys have very little sentimentality about their belongings. Not only is there a difference in how much boys and girls save, there is a difference in what kind of things they keep and how they store them.

Taking these obvious differences into consideration, working with your child toward an organizing solution can and will make organizing much more natural and practical for them. Buying organizing supplies that suit their gender can also create more joy and comfort in their surroundings and help you encourage their growth into a young man or young woman.

How to Use This Book: Finding the Big "O"

When you identify your child's organizing style and determine their sensory preference, learn a little about gender differences, and factor in whether they are an extrovert or introvert, you will

> If we can recognize each child's thinking style and Understand their strengths and weaknesses, we can sculpt a mind at a time.
>
> —Dr. Mel Levine, *A Mind at a Time*

YOUR CHILD'S THINKING STYLE
Organizing Style + Sensory Preference
+ Introvert or Extrovert + Gender

---

be able to dip into this book to find out exactly what to do. You are building a personality profile of your child that goes deep. You are getting the big "O" in organizing that is about self-discovery, which leads to integration, and finally into a better understanding of each other in the world.

Even though it looks like there are several hoops to hop through, it's really very simple and will be enjoyable and fun for you to discover something new about the child in your life. This is a powerful approach to figuring out all your child's organizing needs and concerns, and it should resonate far beyond the limits of this topic. Children come wired with a system that needs to be honored and respected. If you are able to step away from your own needs and focus on what really and truly works for your child, everyone wins. As Stephen Covey suggests, "By organizing your deepest priorities, you're creating alignment and order. You're setting up systems and structures that support—rather than get in the way of—what you're trying to do."

Once you have taken the "What Is Your Child's Thinking Style?" quiz and discovered your child's preference, you can go right to the particular chapter that speaks to his or her identity and begin working with the ideas and suggestions. You will discover strategies that you can put into use after just one sitting. The last chapter offers some special suggestions for today's world, where the traditional nuclear family is no longer the norm, which puts additional organizing challenges on many children. Let's get started.

QUIZ

What Is Your Child's Thinking Style?

Read each statement, and select one answer that most resonates with what your child would do in that given situation. Add up the totals for each letter at the end of the assessment. You'll notice that some of these scenarios might seem a little over the top. They are designed to help you clarify how your child behaves, so exaggeration is sometimes in order. Just have fun imagining what they might do. Practical solutions follow in the next four chapters, one for each thinking style.

1. When your child goes off to summer camp, he/she becomes:
   a. A team player
   b. A teacher's helper
   c. A risk-taker
   d. A goal setter

2. His or her main priority is:
   a. Precision
   b. People
   c. Possibilities
   d. Progress

3. When playing outside, he or she tends to:
   a. Move quickly
   b. Move slowly

c. Motivate others

d. Play by themselves

4. His or her number-one personality trait is:

a. Being organized

b. Helping people

c. Being innovative

d. Being goal-oriented

5. When working on a new science project, he or she:

a. Follows the rules

b. Prefers to have someone help them out

c. Get excited and loses track of time

d. Seriously focuses and hunkers down

6. When it comes to helping you pack for the family summer vacation, he or she will:

a. Pack the exact amount of things

b. Pack what you tell them to bring

c. Pack a variety of unrelated things

d. Let you pack for them

7. Teachers may perceive your child as difficult if he or she:

a. Is unwilling to change

b. Is often chatty

c. Is often moving around a lot

d. Needs to be in control

8. When it comes to handling changes, he or she tends to be:

a. Rigid

b. Worried

    c. Flexible

    d. Logical

9. **When playing with a doll or toy car, he or she focuses on:**

    a. What the instructions say to do

    b. The relationship between the toy and other toys

    c. Creating elaborate fantasies about the toys or people

    d. What function it can perform

10. **His or her energy is:**

    a. Restricted

    b. Generous

    c. Energetic

    d. Repressed

11. **When solving a math problem, he or she approaches it:**

    a. Step by step

    b. With their friends

    c. Creatively

    d. Analytically

12. **A negative report card might reflect the child's:**

    a. Inflexibility

    b. Vulnerability

    c. Independence

    d. Argumentative nature

13. **What drives the child is:**

    a. Following the rules

    b. Approval from peer groups

    c. Freedom to innovate

    d. Achieving goals

14. When comforting a sad friend, he or she is:
   a. A careful listener
   b. Sensitive
   c. Open-minded
   d. Confident

15. If your child becomes irritated, it is best to diffuse the situation by:
   a. Explaining the rules and helping develop a strategy to follow them
   b. Showing that you understand their feelings, talking in a kind way, and then getting off the subject
   c. Showing a sense of humor and being casual, informal, and open-minded to their ideas
   d. Closely listening to their position and building a logical, sound argument

16. The child learns by:
   a. What has been previously done
   b. Working with others
   c. Creative experimenting
   d. Analyzing

17. His or her handwriting tends to be:
   a. Very legible
   b. Attractive
   c. Creative
   d. Minimal

18. In his or her spare time, the child tends to:
   a. Tidy up
   b. Hang out with family/friends

    c. Engage in artistic activities

    d. Fix things

19. **The child's number-one contribution to their classroom is:**

    a. Following rules

    b. Relationships

    c. Creativity

    d. Intellect

20. **The child tends to share their toys when:**

    a. He or she can follow the rules of sharing

    b. He or she likes the friend

    c. He or she can be more creative

    d. He or she can take charge and be in control

21. **Starting at a new school, and depending on extroversion/ introversion qualities, the child tends to be:**

    a. Quiet

    b. Sensitive

    c. Funny

    d. Powerful

22. **Classmates see your child as:**

    a. Following the rules

    b. Friendly

    c. A day dreamer

    d. Competitive

23. **A symbol that might represent your child is:**

    a. A compass

    b. An ocean wave

    c. A bird in the sky

    d. A lightning bolt

24. His or her future occupation could be:

    a. An inspector

    b. A diplomat

    c. An artist or inventor

    d. A decision-maker

25. When building a sand castle, he or she does it with:

    a. Tradition

    b. Feeling

    c. Imagination

    d. Precision

QUIZ RESULTS

*Write the total number of letters circled
in the appropriate columns:*

# of A's circled	# of B's circled	# of C's circled	# of D's circled

This can give you some direction about your child's brain type.

If your child scored:

A's: 13 or more = Maintainer

B's: 13 or more = Harmonizer

C's: 13 or more = Innovator

D's: 13 or more = Prioritizer

If you don't score 13 or higher in any of the categories, it is a good idea for you to read the paragraphs again and compare the child's typical behaviors.

Understanding the Quiz Results

Quizzes can be tricky. Human beings are known for adapting to environments that perpetuate their survival. Even at a young age, children are eager to please and seek our acceptance. I have witnessed some of my client's children, as young as five, copy their mothers in style and mannerisms and follow her in exactly the same manner as she is cleaning the house or baking in the kitchen. Through our rose-colored glasses, it becomes a challenge to truly see what children's natural strengths and challenges are.

Your child may test strong in two thinking styles, and you may have to read both chapters to decide which brain preference they are naturally prone to. Remember that they will only have affinity with one quadrant only. It is your job to know what that is and to build strengths in those and competencies in the others. We never want to be spread out too evenly, with 25 percent of our energy in each quadrant. That would be too energy-intensive. Instead, we want our children to hang out in one of the preferred quadrants as much as possible yet still feel comfortable, for a limited time, in the others.

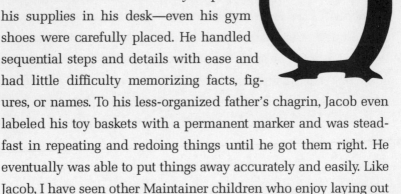

CHAPTER 2

Maintaining Style:
"The Penguin"

> Childhood has its own way of seeing, thinking,
> and feeling, and nothing is more foolish than to
> try to substitute ours for theirs.
> —*Jean-Jacques Rousseau, Emile*

Jacob was a cute little guy of eight years old, as meticulous as he could be. (Perhaps he was a librarian or executive secretary in another life!) At his school, the teachers were shocked to see how neatly he placed his supplies in his desk—even his gym shoes were carefully placed. He handled sequential steps and details with ease and had little difficulty memorizing facts, fig-ures, or names. To his less-organized father's chagrin, Jacob even labeled his toy baskets with a permanent marker and was stead-fast in repeating and redoing things until he got them right. He eventually was able to put things away accurately and easily. Like Jacob, I have seen other Maintainer children who enjoy laying out their school clothes in perfect order each night for the next day!

Your Maintaining-style child is the most into-a-routine per-son of the four thinking styles. Maintainers resemble penguins, those wonderful birds suited up in their uniform white-and-black tuxes, eager to tackle everyday tasks with accuracy, devotion, and a love of structure. Penguins and Maintainers aren't particularly dramatic or flashy, but they know how to commit to the task at hand. Who thought penguins' annual migration to breed was so arduous, as seen in the documentary film, *March of the Penguins*? Just imagine a few dozen well-organized penguins (or Maintainers) marching off to their favorite island ice block in perfect single file. They head up the mound, turn right in unison, and then dive into the water, one after the other, in pristine order. What a wonderfully orchestrated sight to behold! The film's director, Luc Jacquet, said in an interview in *National Geographic* that the penguins "Are easy to work with because they have extremely predictable behavior in terms of what they will be, what they will do, the routes they will take. It's possible to anticipate pretty much everything. You have 3,000 couples [penguins] repeating the same kind of gesture, all at the same moment."

Did you know a penguin can't fly? How unusual and strange for a bird. Well, they may not fly in the air, but they certainly fly through the water! Their wings serve as fins to guide, steer, and maneuver them through all kinds of conditions. They are such steady eddies, committed to one another and the plan at hand, as they propel themselves through mellow or turbulent waters, always loyal to their current agenda. That is a focus the penguin and the Maintainer share—the ability and unflinching skill to hold the course, and the commitment to complete the task, no matter how daunting.

Penguins also have the uncanny ability to jump right out of the water and land on the ground, right on their own webbed feet. Pretty impressive, but who would know such a thing? Penguins and Maintainers don't show off, but they do achieve great things and take themselves and their projects quite seriously. Consider the penguin as mate and parent. They are very devoted and remain faithful to their partners for months on end while scouring the terrain looking for food. They also provide great stability for their offspring by being extremely on-task and vigilant parents. When the penguin egg is laid, the father carries it on his feet so it does not touch the ice for more than two months while he waits, totally focused until the egg hatches. He barely moves, doesn't eat (he loses about twenty pounds), and stays huddled with the other male penguins, completely consumed by his responsibility. When the egg hatches, the mother takes over all the parenting duties and keeps an eye out for her baby for four solid years. That's devotion!

Penguins don't usually act erratically. These stable birds seem to know what they are going to do next and rarely engage in sudden or unplanned behaviors. Just like the Maintaining-style child, the penguin thrives with predictability and familiar routines. Urgency, pressure, and a loud, "Get it done right now!" doesn't work well with these children. They will feel stressed out and deeply alarmed if they cannot take the time to plan and organize their next move. They need organization and structure to guide their life, day in and day out.

Jacob likes being on time and expects everyone else to show up on the dot, too. He made sure he was meticulously dressed in his new suit and tie hours before his big brother's bar mitzvah. Because he was giving a speech at the event, he made sure it was written three weeks in advance and he rehearsed it daily. Obviously, respecting and honoring time and commitments is very important to Jacob. He gets stressed out when he cannot prepare for each and every activity or project in the day—no surprises for this Maintainer! Jacob feels comforted knowing what is expected of him and enjoys making his family proud by having everything in order.

The last time Jacob's family took a camping trip, his older sister forgot the flashlight, his older brother forgot his fishing rod, and his parents forgot insect repellent! Instead of hiking and having fun, the first day of the trip was spent shopping for supplies. Ten-year-old Jacob was frustrated, threw his hands in the air, and proclaimed, "Enough is enough." One week before their next summer vacation, he composed a thorough checklist for each member of the family. At first they balked. How could they let a kid boss them around? But his parents knew Jacob could deal with details and applauded his giftedness. Their next trip to the woods was more fun for everyone; nothing was forgotten, and Jacob felt safe, secure, and happy.

At school, Jacob enjoys the routine and structure of school. He gets his assignments in on time, and his teachers appreciate his punctuality and work ethic. On the last day of class, his teacher handed out a long list of supplies for next year. In midsummer, when office supply stores gear up for the school year, Jacob insisted his mother drive him to the store to purchase supplies. He unfolded his list and took delight in choosing papers, rulers, and pencils. Then he neatly organized all his supplies into his new backpack and hung it on a hook by the back door a good month before the first day of fifth grade.

Jacob likes playing board games over physical activities. He enjoys Monopoly and loves being the banker because this role allows him to know and enforce the rules. Jacob prefers the structure and predictability involved in going around the board, collecting money, and putting houses on the properties. It isn't that he wanted to control the environment, but he thrives when he's micromanaging and making the best use of his talents. He may not be the most risk-taking or fun friend, but his buddies like playing with him because they knew he would follow the rules and, more importantly, to some, none of the pieces of the game would be missing.

The Maintainer child is usually a natural planner and team player, but throw them a curve—present them with something new—and he or she may freeze up for a moment or two. Anything out of the ordinary requires them to stop and think; then, in their methodical, step-by-step manner, they will carefully consider what to do next. They need security and balance. They also love convention and willingly embrace the regularity of family events and traditional holidays. You'll be amazed as they run off to make their calendar during the summertime when you remind them you'll be off to Grandma's house for Christmas, five months down the road!

In many ways, Maintainers are devoted to their family and do as they are told if you can explain exactly what you want them to do. From cleaning out the garage to organizing the address book, they will try their utmost to complete the task. They aren't the type to complain and feel a sense of pride in accomplishing all chores around the home, including keeping their room in order.

Maintainers prefer tasks that require structure and order and can be challenged when anything out of the ordinary happens. Because life is change, be prepared to give them extra help and support as they learn how to maneuver the ups and downs of growing up.

The Maintainer's Thinking Style

> #58—Neatness, accuracy, attention to detail.
> —Catharine M. Cox,
> *Early Mental Traits of Three Hundred Geniuses*

Thank goodness for all our remarkable Maintainers. Without them, this world would be more of a mess. Who would complete and deliver projects on time? Who would be sure to plan ahead? Who would break down a task into doable steps and plow ahead until everything was neat and accurate? Of course, along with the drive to be thorough and orderly is a need to keep things predictable and routine. Don't think that they will excite you with new ideas or unconventional strategies. Quite the contrary. Their interests and conversations revolve around what they have heard or read and the things that have already been accomplished.

Maintainers learn through trial and error, like most other children, but they are generally more comfortable when they have step-by-step, how-to instructions. No surprises, please! Naturally, they prefer to know what to expect before they act. If your child is a Maintainer, you will need to offer plenty of support and assurance before he or she is willing to try anything new. They really excel when things in their environment are in order and easy for them to use. They do not do well when their stuff is handled, misplaced, or lost. Your Maintainer does not easily share books or toys. It's not because they aren't kind; it's just because they know things can be mistreated, and they really aren't too flexible when a book comes back torn or a toy is returned broken.

How can you utilize their preference for order and commitment to completion? Have them help you make lists of what you need to take on a trip, what you need to do to prepare for an up-coming event, or what to buy to make that fancy birthday cake. They prefer to list all the necessary steps to accomplish a project and are able to focus on the details. So enjoy this wonderful child who tends to follow the rules if you explain them clearly and write them down to boot. After they are told what to do and how to do it, they are full speed ahead. They tend to finish jobs on time and in good order—and that includes homework!

Because they are cautious, methodical, and careful workers, Maintainers can usually handle activities that require fine motor activities. Watch them and delight in their precision especially in arts and crafts as they color inside the lines, cut out items accu-rately, glue sequins carefully onto fabric—you name it! Remem-ber, they aren't speed demons and work methodically, but they usually complete a task!

How Maintainers function is a testament to the power of or-ganization and the comfort and self-assurance it gives them. They are the type of children who receive the school supply list for the next grade at the end of the year, and can't wait to get everything they need months before classes begin in the fall and their school backpack maybe ready to go weeks in advance.

If you are the parent of a Maintainer child, you are lucky in that these children innately love to organize and help out around the house. The following list of qualities and traits describe the many facets of a typical Maintaining-style child. These are not meant to pigeonhole him or her into a limited set of definitions, but rather to paint a bigger picture, to open your eyes to many of your child's particular gifts and talents. Notice how you view these traits. Some might seem negative at first read, so take a mo-ment and consider the positive side as well. For example, *cautious* might seem restrictive. Think again and you'll realize it also means "aware" and "attentive." Knowing more about who your child is and how he or she ticks will inform and inspire new ways to communicate and relate with your Maintainer child.

Qualities and Traits of the Maintaining-Style Child

> Such disorder I never saw in all my days.
> If people are fools enough to let their grass grow long, they should have the decency to braid it.
>
> —Anne Lindbergh and Susan Hoguet,
> *Tidy Lady*

- Cautious
- Detailed
- Exact
- Factual
- Follows directions
- Industrious
- Orderly
- Persistent

- Practical
- Predictable
- Realistic
- Reliable
- Task-driven
- Thorough
- Uncluttered

When you read these words and recognize traits you see in your Maintainer child, such as predictable and task-driven, you will be able to really identify and support the qualities of living that will help your child be who he or she is, without criticism or confusion. A practical and task-driven child, for example, needs a specific kind of environment and treatment to thrive. The more you understand your Maintainer child, the better you will be at creating a relationship that is more accepting and less intimidating, where they are able to feel safe and be willing to try *slightly* new things. This is an important point, as it will truly contribute to their growth and expansion as they grow up.

How "the Penguin" Relates to Time

> Children love structure—it gives them freedom.
>
> —Dr. Edward Hallowell,
> *The Childhood Roots of Adult Happiness*

When it comes to keeping track of time and scheduling, Maintainers flourish. As you know, they appreciate routine and want to keep track of every activity. Time anchors them and makes them produce and move forward. They can meet deadlines and are even likely to include them when they are making music or coloring a picture. They like to keep their eyes on the clock even when coloring and tend to get things done in a timely manner. Chances are that they will also show up early for classes or appointments or even dinner. Punctuality and the Maintaining style go hand-in-hand.

The Maintaining-style child likes to "get it done" and "do it right." Time doesn't hinder them or create angst but works for them and supports their efforts. These children thrive with structured time: dinner, homework, and bed happen at the same time every day, week in and week out. If you are able to give them some form of consistency, they will be more confident at home and at school. Of the four thinking styles, Maintainers need a more rigid schedule and even block out the hours for their weekends.

They rarely focus on the big picture, like the Innovating child, but eagerly jot down all the specifics on a to-do list. It may not look official, but truth be told, it gives them an anchor in their day and makes them happy as they check off task after task. They also like putting up weekly activity charts in their bedroom and creating grids for homework pages in their schoolbooks.

They conform easily to a schedule and may only need a little guidance and support from their main caregiver. For example, when Tuesday is ballet and Thursday is piano, they want to know the plan for how to get to their lesson, what to take, and when. They like to know that they will be picked up from school, have a quick snack at home, and that special ballet clothes or piano music they need are stored in a nice container in the trunk of the car.

When they are fixated on a special project, they may go that extra mile. Don't look for any multitasking when your Maintainer is on task. They can sit still for long periods of time and have an extraordinary ability to stay focused and concentrate. If they tend to be more introverted, try not to interrupt them, because the time they have dedicated to this work is meaningful and important.

What are some ways you can support your Maintainer child's talents? Let them set up a chore chart, on which they can assign the duty and the day it needs to be done to each member of the family. Of course, you will be governing those choices, but let them track completion. They also enjoy taking the minutes at family meetings or planning the agenda. Give them that sense of power, and they will think that their talents are very valued and eventually become very skilled at them. Ultimately, you will encourage them to flourish in what they instinctually do well, and by respecting and honoring their talents, give them ways to shine.

A couple time management staples can be extremely beneficial to your Maintaining child. Even though some schools provide their students with a calendar that goes through the school year, it may not be as specific as your child needs. Take your child to a large stationery store and have them pick out an organizer, planner, or agenda book. Perhaps you may see this as unnecessary, as they just are in the second grade and only have a couple lessons during the week. However, it is comforting for them to know what is happening on certain days, even if there are few things going on. Developing organizing skills early in your child's life will make way for fewer complications in the future. They also have the tendency to write small and very legibly, so a big monthly calendar will not work. They need to write down the details and have hourly placements to record their next activity. You may want to get them a calendar for the summer months as well, to keep track of travels and adventures.

Because they are very keen on time and feel anxious when they aren't sticking to a schedule, they usually often like getting to events way ahead of time. A client of mine has a Maintainer child named Jennifer who is in grade three. She loves going to the movies but implores her parents over and over to get to the theater at least fifteen minutes early, as she may need to go to the rest room or buy a soda. She doesn't like going into the theater when it is dark but likes to walk in and sit down, safe and comfortable, before unexpected things pop up on the big screen!

The Maintaining-style child does like helping others, but sometimes at too great a personal cost. Their own downtime is crucial for their well-being. It rejuvenates them, but often they won't schedule any time for themselves as they run around to make sure all the tasks in the household are completed. Help them schedule their own private time into their busy day, and be sure you honor them and give them some alone time when they need it or ask for it.

Maintainers can be seen as being very rigid. After a plan is laid down, they prefer not to change it. It can be a challenge helping them understand the need for flexibility about scheduling. If someone changes a plan at the last minute, be prepared for some serious frustration on the part of your Maintainer. Respect your child's relationship with time instead of imposing your own. This can help build an atmosphere of support and health. If you are able to be more conscious about how you handle time, if you are able to put some effort into following some routines, and if you recognize that change for them is a bit of a trauma, you can help them feel balanced and safe.

The Maintalner at Home

Maintainer children need a practical and realistic home life. They don't respond well to unconventional ideas or highly emotional words or expectations. It is important you learn how to speak their language. When you do, they will feel safe, nurtured, and whole. Obviously, the better you two communicate, the easier it is for you to instruct and guide them into doing things that will help them grow into solid, confident adults.

Ask your Maintaining child where last year's Halloween costumes are, and they probably will know! They are apt to put things back to their proper place. In their bedroom, have their own special place for everything. All their CDs, computer games

> She thought a bit. Then she said, "There is
> nothing more orderly than the alphabet.
> Everything I have begins with one letter or
> another. I'll just put it all in the order of the
> ABC's.
>
> —Ellen Kindt McKenzie and Megan Lloyd,
> *The Perfectly Orderly House*

or books are in order, and their stuffed animals may be on the floor but in the same spot only when they are sleeping. They care about the appearance of the home, never mind their own appearance, and don't like things to get too messy or even dirty. They like themselves, their things, and others to be clean and well organized. That is the gift they give to everyone.

Maintaining children are usually easy to live with and aren't terribly demanding. Chances are that they would willingly even eat the same type of food every day of the week as long as it was tasty. A Maintaining child I worked with named Lauren, even in grade one, would do her hair every day in a little ponytail with two hair clips placed perfectly even on either side of her head. She would plan out her entire wardrobe, making sure her shoes and socks matched. (Quite unlike some other children I know.)

Maintainers tend to take responsibility very seriously and will act in an appropriate manner. They will tend to follow your exact directions and instructions and won't have the desire to change anything. They appreciate etiquette and manners and are poised and determined. A client of mine in Los Angeles asked me to help plan her son's bar mitzvah. At such a young age, thirteen, he came prepared to the initial meeting with a list of invitees, what the theme was going to be, the schedule of events, and even what the main course was going to be! I said to myself, "A budding professional organizer in my midst." His mother said he was like this from day one.

Give Maintainers privacy in their own room, and create enough space for them to get some privacy. They dislike their personal space being invaded. They need their space, and not to share, if possible. (Only if they are introverted. If extroverted, they may want to be playing on a team a lot!) They are not necessarily laid back, but nonetheless, they need space. Peace for them is having privacy.

Some minor challenges you may face include the fact that they are creatures of habit and don't like others to touch or even move their things. They may become upset if something of theirs is moved or broken. Sometimes they don't want to share things with their siblings or friends. A young boy, Kedric, in the fourth grade had the hardest time when his parents downsized and called me in to rearrange their kids' rooms. Now Kedric had to share his space with his younger brother. He wasn't too happy, as his younger brother enjoyed playing with his older brother's stuff. Maintainers usually have an enormous sense of propriety and tend to share only if things won't get broken.

They may have some tunnel vision if you want things to be changed and done differently. Chances are that they will need to be encouraged to do anything that hasn't been done before. If that is the least of your worries, no problem; it could be much worse. Be sensible, they appreciate that, and show them some past success or invoke a reasonable rule, and they will be willing to learn how to do something that is new and perhaps not anything like they have done before.

Also, as the caregiver, it would be great if you could leave

things in order. Order is not trivial to Maintainers. Chances are
they will be critical of your every move and the best way to not
upset them or make them feel uncomfortable is to keep things in
reasonable order. When you have a hard time, ask them to help
out; they would be more than willing. Or with size, for example,
pick up the larger stuffed animal, then the next smallest, and so
on until they have them all picked up.

Once they know that they are trusted, and their approach to
what they want out of life is respected and even honored, Maintainers can flourish. They love to accept responsibility and feel
good about it. When they sense that they are valued, they will be
your next in command. They will be industrious and a committed team player when shown the way. Their reliability and mas-
tering what you tell them to do will give you a sense of security
and comfort knowing that they are safe and sound. Ultimately,
they want to feel like they are a valuable member to the household and like to live by a daily routine as much as possible. Like
all children who need structure and balance, Maintainers truly
come alive and thrive in a home environment that has structure
and is well organized.

The Maintainer at School

Chances are, you are probably raising the next potential copy editor, accountant, assembly line worker, service worker, or attorney
when it comes to the future job possibilities of the Maintaining
style. They tend to adapt to school because they enjoy structured
learning. They also take school seriously, pay attention to the
teacher, and focus on all their tasks and assignments. "This is no
time to fool around," they might say. They like a teacher who

> There is a relationship between a clean,
> well-organized home and the educational and
> financial success of the children who grew up
> there.
>
> —Jay Davidson, *Teach Your Children Well*

prefers regular routines, and the teacher likes them, as they don't challenge them and get their homework in on time. They don't like to waste time, and they do well with the intense short focus of classes and regimented day plan. They turn in legible homework time and time again and enjoy making their parents and teachers proud. Maintainers are successful students!

Maintainers excel during the first years of schooling, known as the "grammar stage," because memorizing words and numbers and learning structures and forms come quite easily for them. They thrive on routine, regularity, and knowing what is expected of them. Coming up with imaginative answers, filling in the blanks on a pop quiz, or crafting creative essays aren't their cup of tea. These tasks require too much innovative thinking or the ability to handle surprise. Maintainers prefer true/false exams and straightforward subjects that deal with phonics, grammar, charts, and graphs. They may excel at reading, enjoy language, and are fascinated with words. For example, when they are in a car, they may pay more attention to the words on the passing billboards than the scenery!

Here's a really important tip: try not to get in their way! Because their work style is very quiet and consistent, Maintainers truly dislike to be interrupted. They like to keep their nose to the grindstone and come up for air when they are finally done. They like to give 100 percent to every project or assignment and will work hard to do things right. They are competent, studious, and serious.

The Maintaining-style child loves to be organized, in the traditional sense. Be sure you provide them with utilitarian solutions, including a two-drawer filing cabinet, with hanging files, and folders that are either organized by class or projects. Nothing too fancy; the more user friendly the better. Buy simple manila file folders, green hanging files, and clear, plastic 2-inch tabs, about 25 for each drawer. Give them their own labeler (do you have one?), and they will be in heaven! (It would probably make a great birthday gift for them.) If they are too young to use a labeler, give them stickers and a nice pen. Don't worry; this is not a waste of your time or money. These children will use their filing cabinet with ease and delight! Next, be sure your Maintainer's school backpack has a main compartment for books and several side compartments to store highlighters, pens, and pencils. They like to have their supplies with them at all times. Buy another set for their home desk.

If the school no longer allows backpacks in the classroom, help your child make their own pen and pencil container to keep at school. These supplies make your Maintainer feel safe and secure. Try not to borrow a pen from them and forget to return it. This is most unnerving for these kids! At home, create a regular space dedicated to your Maintainer's homework. It can be in their bedroom, at the dining room or kitchen table, anywhere, really, as long as it is consistent. However, if you can give them a desk in their bedroom, they will go wild with joy! Don't forget to dedicate a cubbyhole or basket for all their permission slips and homework assignments that you can check before they go to school in the morning.

A couple things could easily challenge them as they get on in their school years. For example, if a history project is too big, help them break it down into workable stages, and assign deadlines to each part of the project. Maintainers are not big-picture thinkers and are overwhelmed if they cannot see the baby steps to get from A to Z. Like most children who have a very busy school life, Maintainers are natural planners and will feel more self-assured if they know what the next step is. Remember, no surprises for them!

They also may need more time to adjust to new schools, teachers, and friends. Anything that is out of the ordinary makes them feel uncertain, scared, and withdrawn. Give them time to warm up to new situations, and let them come out of their shell when they are ready. School adjustments can be traumatic for anyone, and moving from one classroom in primary school to six classrooms in middle school can be intimidating. Spend extra time with them; explain to them the changes and where things are in their new school. Take it slow.

Third, because they like routines and can find new situations challenging, they may initially appear more introverted than they actually are. Some of the other kids might find them a tad too serious, and they may not make friends quickly. Luckily, they like and respect teachers and are willing team players. If they take the lead, some kids may not appreciate how strict they are. They just want everyone to follow the rules.

The Penguin at Play

Play is the work of all children, but they just approach it in different ways. As young children, the Maintaining-style child really enjoys being alone to do his or her own thing. That pretty much

> The universe will change if you bring up your
> children, not in the freedom of the libertine,
> but in behaviorist freedom.
>
> —John Broadus Watson,
> *Behaviorism, 12—Bartlett's Familiar Quotations*

sums it up. They are masters at entertaining themselves and enjoy stamp collecting, crossword puzzles, and cards games. They thrive at mental, not physical, games. Horsing around and running and wrestling don't really thrill them, and any big birthday party where children are playing wild and crazy games actually creates a lot of discomfort.

They prefer activities that are more quiet and less active. Because they thrive in team sports, not individualistic adventurous sports, they aren't that big into being physical, or play sports, they aren't sissies; rather they just aren't that adventurous. They may make good Boy Scouts or Girl Scouts, but within a structured, authoritarian environment, they could be a bit more social yet still feel that their true selves are being honored. They would rather have little physical contact and prefer to use their mind to create and have some fun. They will become part of the team if it is structured and it is presented well to them. They would do well in dance classes or team sports, as long as they are able to see the finish line, like a dance recital or year-end game. That works for them and would make it fun, yet comfortable.

An excess of toys and games isn't going to make them that happy. They need fewer, but more complicated, intricate toys to open their mind and their understanding of the world. They could sit and play with a train set for a very long time, putting things together and then taking them part and watching the train go around and around. They may add something to the scenery or take things away. But all in all, they are by themselves and loving it!

Some children may view them as stuck in the mud. Because they are very serious and prefer not to deviate from the rules and expectations of teachers and parents, they may not be that fun to hang around with. Everything they do, even off hours, needs to have an objective, something they can check off and feel good about. They need some completing, a sense of major accomplishment when working away. They prefer no interruptions, little sharing and no "challenging the status quo." They get so stirred up if a piece of a puzzle is missing or something is broken that they care not to share with anyone. They may enjoy collecting things (e.g., coins, stamps, cards). They prefer to be able to use their methodical side in the fun things they do.

Let's face it: Maintainer kids like to read books about the real world and stories about how people did things. They like to keep it real, clean, and honest. After they know the rules to a game, or have a played a game before, they are able to feel confident. They need to feel safe and secure before they leap up and be courageous. Give them in-depth explanations, and they will feel confident to move ahead.

When playing with other children, they can appear a bit controlling if things aren't done according to the rules. "You should do this" and "why don't you do it like this" may not endear them to others but can help keep a team in line. They like to keep records of whose turn it was last, and chances are they will keep score when playing cards or any game. They are usually fair and honest.

Sometimes other children may not want to play with them,

for not just the lack of imagination, but rather because they think there is only one way to play a game or to solve a problem. They are usually kind and sincere in explaining to their friends the best possible way to do something. They tend to be rigid because they believe there is only one way, and one right way, to do things.

The Maintaining-style child can seem reserved and not that emotionally connected to those around them. As they like to do just one thing at a time, sometimes there is too much stimulation and uncertainty for them and it makes them uncomfortable. They may seem nerdy or studious to other children. They may be critical of others errors or when others disrespect the rules of a game or do things their own way.

They ultimately need to know the reason behind games, how to win, and how to do better. They like to be seen as fair and as competent. They don't appreciate being made fun of and teased. If they can move around and play games and enjoy activities that let them feel like they are part of something, they will be committed to that arena.

Nurturing Your Maintaining-Style Child

> Each day of our lives we make deposits in the
> memory banks of our children.
> —Charles R. Swindoll, *www.stresslesscountry.com*

All in all, Maintaining-style children aim to please. They are happy when they know they have done a job or task right, and they feel good knowing what they do benefits others. Their desire is to help makes things easier for everyone and implement routines that allow them to manage their surroundings, which make them feel safe and secure. They have reasonably good manners—they are still kids, don't forget—and rarely act in reckless unconventional ways. They don't like surprises, always wanting to know what is coming around the corner before they might run into it.

Maintainers are the most structured of the four thinking styles as well as the most tenacious. You have a hard worker on your hands. Enjoy their tenacity, and respect their needs. Think before you speak, and gather your thoughts about what you expect. They like things to be predictable and will do what is required of them, but they definitely do not think out of the box. Their main talent is that they usually complete any task, with minimal errors and on time. They thrive on that.

For the Maintainer child, the urge to be organized is an innate part of their personality. For the rest out there, organizing is often a low priority. Like a fish needs water, Maintainers need to be organized. They want to be appreciated for their orderly abilities and skills. How can you help them? Give them exact directions when you ask them to do something, set specific limits, and be specific about future plans. Don't embellish and exaggerate the points you share. Be attentive when you ask them to do something and then wait for them to react. "Please pick up the T-shirt from the floor and put in your dirty clothes basket." Wait until they do it, making sure it goes in the hamper. They may need to only be told once, as they are prone to form habits very quickly.

You can also speak their language by giving them lists and letting them help decide what goes on that list. Make a game out of it, and they will think it is cool and will have a fun time doing it. You can even take it to one more level: encourage them to interview adults about how they plan their day and then give them a day planner and help them schedule their time on their own. Your Maintainer will also be delighted to make a pocket organizer that includes to-do lists and important contact information. They will be flattered and honored to be in charge of the family calendar, on which they can add items and remind people of what is coming up. When you have a family meeting, annually or monthly, let them take notes and be the secretary of the event. They will keep consistent and accurate notes and will even prepare a file organized to reflect the year's meetings!

Lastly, and most importantly, the Maintaining-style child does not seek compliments but really thrives when they're noticed and honored for all they do. They are often ignored and not acknowledged because they are quietly practical and task-oriented and not flashy or demanding. As parents and caregivers, this is where you can make an outstanding contribution to your child's sense of value and self-worth. When your Maintainer is appreciated and supported, they truly thrive. As you begin to understand their natural gifts and talents, you will be able to create an environment that supports them living true to their style. This will provide them with a healthy sense of self-awareness and well-being. Begin today and affirm specifically what your child does well. Mention their positive strengths in front of their peers or people that they admire and you'll see them smile.

How about taking this one step further? Maintainers love tangible rewards. Give them special certificates, ribbons, or trophies to honor their achievements, and they'll put them in a special place, admire them, and dust them off with pride. Other ways to express your appreciation would be the gift of heirloom toys or how-to books. Remember, they love to help out, and knowing that they made a difference can give them confidence, reinforce their natural talents, and provide them with enough focus that they are able to repeat this over and over again, proving to themselves and others that they have emerged triumphant.

Maintaining Style: Overview

Purpose: To provide consistency, reliability, and stability for themselves and for others.

Organization of space: They like things to be "just so." They are the quintessential organizers in the making whose motto is "a place for everything, and everything in its place."

Strengths: They are great helpers in labeling and putting things away. Maintainers also want to assist their family and friends on all tasks.

Challenges: Not apt to try new things without a lot of preparation.

Maintaining Style: Time

Calendar: Needs to know what is expected of them and what they need to do at all times. Works well with a basic calendar. Provide plenty of room for them to write in activities, even on the weekends!

To-do list: Enjoys making lists and checking things off when completed.

Goals: Punctuality and doing it right.

Maintaining Style: Home

Bedroom: Spends extra time to be sure belongings are neat and in order. Meticulous quality in arranging things, down to size, color, and function.

Memorabilia: Takes good care of special possessions and keeps them for a long time. Things are well organized, clean, and labeled.

Strengths: Likes to use containers to hold cherished possessions. Maintainers are willing to give things away once they know the particulars about why and have preplanned how much stuff they plan to keep.

Challenges: Likes to have things just so and dedicates time alone, away from friends and family, to keeping order. Not very flexible about change and often unwilling to compromise their standards of quality to work with others.

Maintaining Style: School

Homework: Prefers working at the same time and place every single day. Dislikes being rushed and does not work well under pressure. Hands in assignments on time.

Strengths: Loves details, is an excellent speller, and has neat penmanship. Willing and eager to follow directions.

Challenges: Doesn't like creative problem-solving. May have difficultly with assignments when directions are vague.

Easy Ways to Get Your Maintainer Child Organized

- Respect and appreciate their need to get organized. Make organizing a family topic of conversation, and give them center stage to offer ideas and suggestions.
- Be mindful of their need to be on time. Put up a dry-erase board or calendar in their room, and encourage them to keep track of upcoming holidays and school deadlines.
- Purchase utilitarian organizing supplies, and give them their very own labeler! They will love it.
- They enjoy arranging objects. Be specific and limit what area they should do first.
- Give them a place in their bedroom, even the floor, where they can lay out their clothes the night before school.
- Be specific where things go in their room. They are more than likely to return them to their proper home.
- Help them prioritize. Because they tend to keep a lot, not just for emotional reasons like the Harmonizer, give value to what is important, or has lots of importance, or is not that important.
- Create a checklist for vacations, sleepovers, school, or any other activity that requires packing or having supplies ready.
- They dislike interruptions. When they are working, leave them be, or create a sign for them to put on their bedroom door when they are working on their homework or a project.
- Let them know in advance what is happening or if any changes are going to be made. Remember, they don't like surprises.

CHAPTER 3

Harmonizing Style:
"The Dog"

I can't find my bear. I asked my mother, "Did you
see my bear?" "I can't help you now."
  I said to my father, "I can't find my bear, will
you help me?" And he said, "You are always los-
ing things. I want you to find it for yourself and
that will be a lesson to you, to remember where
you put things."
  "Nobody will help me find my bear." So I
cried and nobody stopped me.
— Jules Feiffer, *I Lost My Bear*

Alexis was a people-pleaser from day one.
She was more concerned about what others were
thinking than about her own feelings. For example, if
she was talking on the phone to one of her girlfriends
who was upset, Alexis would keep talking until
her friend felt better, even if her family was
waiting on her to go out to dinner. Alexis
could easily read nonverbal signals. She
was dedicated to promoting the peace and
always made everyone feel welcome and
comfortable when they came to visit her in her bedroom. Naturally
a collector of many things, Alexis's environment was always upbeat
and colorful, and she always had more than enough of everything.

To help her feel comfortable that all was well in her world, she would look at or play with all the things she collected, and she would find herself feeling connected and happy. One day Alexis's mother asked me for some organizational help with her own paperwork, and that's when I noticed that Alexis's mementos and numerous dance trophies were starting to crowd her out of her little bedroom. I offered some organizing tips to help her mother gently enforce limits as to how much Alexis could keep each year. We devised creative ways to keep her memories alive without cluttering the entire house. Alexis didn't like to organize much until we all did it together, as a team. At last, Alexis has learned to live with a reasonable amount of stuff and occasionally has a purging/slumber party with all her girlfriends to help her sort through the ever-accumulating boxes of stuff.

Your Harmonizing-style child tends to be the most loyal, sensitive, and helpful of the four thinking styles. They can be great companions because they are typically caring and emotionally supportive to family, friends, and everyone who is lucky enough to cross their path. What kind of animal does this child sound like? The devoted dog, of course, the most popular pet in the world! Harmonizers and dogs share so many attributes. They are giving by nature and want to be in service. With the dog's keen sense of smell and skill at providing vision for those who are blind, and with the Harmonizer's intuition and skill at reading nonverbal expressions and nuances, both have the ability to sense what is happening around them, always on the lookout to be sure family and friends feel happy, safe, and taken care of.

Just like the numerous breeds, from watchdogs to hunters, retrievers to herders, dogs and Harmonizers are devoted to pleasing others in every possible way, and both easily adapt to all kinds of people and situations. Just watch as your Harmonizer mirrors the gestures, mannerisms, and behaviors of those around them, not only for fun, but also as a way to connect and build rapport. They are very aware of what is happening all around them and are concerned with everyone they come into contact with. If you're happy, they're happy!

It is no surprise that the image of the dog shows up near and far. Respected animals whose visage symbolizes qualities all of us revere, the dog was the guardian of the sacred tombs in Ancient Greece; the protector for the rich and powerful in early Rome; messengers and servants to the priesthood in Christian antiquity; and in India, Native American tradition, and almost all cultures, dogs appear as almost saintly or angelic beings. Certainly the dog continues to be our best friend!

Dogs and Harmonizers are faithful and give their family a sense of unconditional love and companionship. Dogs and Harmonizers get terribly lonesome when their loved ones are not around. Both share a pack mentality, and they need people to help them feel alive. When a Harmonizing-style child says, "I'm bored. There is nothing to do," chances are they are actually feeling lonesome. They need to be connected and needed. The Harmonizer is capable of deep feelings and enormous compassion. Their purpose is to build trust, harmony, and peaceful foundations. They are also unselfish and want everyone to be happy. Because they tend to be optimistic, playful, fun-loving, and adaptable to almost any situation, they are often the first to offer help and encouragement to others.

Let's face it: Alexis is always running a bit late. Even when she knows well in advance what time to get ready for school, she is still behind. Instead of getting frustrated, her mother designed a perfectly beautiful "Harmonizer" calendar, filled with color and charm, and hung it up on her bedroom door where Alexis could always see it. She was encouraged to make any changes or additions to it throughout the day. Her mother also bought a set of plastic numbers and taped the time for her daily appointments and classes on the door as well! Alexis loved the big numbers, which helped her connect with when she needed to be at school or her playdate.

Alexis has saved every greeting card anyone has given her over her long eight years as well as everything else she holds dear. Purging is tough for this Harmonizer. Her mother decided she needed help and invited Alexis's best friend over to be part of a "purge party." Her mom bought a scrapbook and stickers and glue and left Alexis and Rachel alone with all the stuff piled high. Rachel helped Alexis put all her cards into one book, instead of crammed in a box underneath the bed, and the two of them laughed and applauded as they went through page by page! They made an agreement that from now on, Alexis would buy scrapbooks for all her odds and ends, and the next sleepover she could share her bounty by bringing them out to entertain her friends.

Alexis loves school because it is the place to connect with friends and have fun. But when it comes to remembering what books to bring to class or home, she often falls short. She'd never forget a friend's birthday party, though! Her mom helped her put together a set of binders to jog her memory. The green binder was English, and the green book covers wrapped around her reading books. The blue binder was science, and all her science books were covered in blue, too. Because Alexis loves and connects with colors, she now feels happier and more organized as she lines up her beautiful rainbow of class binders.

Alexis enjoys acting and performing. When her friends get together, the gang can go all night doing puppet shows, dancing, and performing for one another. She loves a party and is happiest when a ton of friends come over and they can dress up and sing and laugh. Alexis has collected a variety of costumes and keeps all of them, even the ones she has outgrown. She also hoards doll clothes, props, and piles of toys. Her mother has realized these things are meaningful to her daughter and built a little extra stand-up closet right in the corner of the room, dedicated especially to party-time props.

The Harmonizing-style child is motivated by social recognition and the need for companionship. Their focus is more on connection and relating and less on how well things are working. Obviously, organizing isn't their cup of tea. Because they aren't detail oriented, particularly efficient, or bossy, their approach to getting things "together" tends to be rather spontaneous. Let's face it: they need a lot of help to de-clutter. No worries, though. With your help, they'll learn a few organizing tricks, and like the dog, will be eager to show you what they know!

Sometimes the Harmonizing child gives more to others than they give to themselves. This can be both an asset and a detriment. I have a client whose Harmonizer daughter is always helping her friends do their homework before she does her own. She so wants to help out, and in the process, ends up turning her reports in late! Just a tip: if you hang around your Harmonizer while they do their homework, they'll do it better and with more confidence to boot! But don't expect them to speed up. They like to take their time and smell the roses!

You can support their special thinking style and respect their talents by building a home that feels safe, happy, and warm.

Everything they do is to connect with others, for example their use of the computer, whether to see the latest photos from your last family trip, or to e-mail Aunty Sarah about the latest experience. When they find their comfort zone, they'll be eager to follow your lead as you help them organize their rooms and their lives.

Thinking Style

> "In a quiet room a dreaming dog wagged his tail. A fuzzy cat snoozed. A plump hamster napped in a shoe. And a sleepy parakeet whistled on the bedpost. 'I can't clean my room,' a child whispered to his mother. 'All the animals are sleeping. I'll clean it later.'"
>
> —Lisa Westberg Peters and Brad Sneed,
> *When the Fly Flew In . . .*

The Harmonizing child learns best when they are in close physical proximity with other people. They get a lot out of watching your every move and then following through imitating you most of the time. Your complete, undivided attention for even ten quality minutes will make them feel happy. Because they are people-centered and very personable, they are sensitive to the feelings of others. They learn best when they are emotionally comforted and feel taken care of.

Harmonizers are extremely aware of and sensitive to non-verbal communication. There are more than 70,000 movements and gestures you make with your face and body, expressions you convey without words, that communicate all kinds of nuances of sensation and emotion. Don't be surprised if your Harmonizer child picks up most of them! How does this revelation translate into something practical?

Harmonizers respond to more than the content of what you say. They are influenced by tone of voice, posture, and whether you are smiling or not. So when you ask them to put away their clothes, be conscious of how you express yourself. Try to avoid standing with your hands on your hips in what can be construed as a confrontational pose, and use a tone that is diplomatic and nonthreatening. You might think you are simply being direct and what's the big deal, but your sensitive Harmonizer might feel an undercurrent or edginess in your demeanor. Maybe you are just tired, but they will take it personally. So embrace this challenge; couch your words with extra kindness, and know your child will feel loved, honored, and willing to help in every way.

The Harmonizing child tends to talk, talk, and talk while they work or play. They can be a bit dramatic and are known to embellish when telling stories. It's fun for them to come alive with passion and joy as they express themselves, in dance or expressive movement, preferably in front of an audience. Like the dog, they want to feel loved and needed, and they usually enjoy being held, stroked, and hugged. They love to touch back, too. So add a little eye contact and a couple soft words of praise, and the dog and Harmonizer will be eagerly wagging their tails and probably won't sit until you are there with them.

Harmonizers tend to follow the rules of the specific environment in which they find themselves. But they often feel most comfortable at home or in a familiar situation. As Dr. Taylor suggests, "They may be fairly consistent about implementation of habits when within their immediate environment and somewhat inconsistent about implementation if outside their immediate environment or if others change their habits." The bottom line is this: Harmonizers tend to want to fit in with their peers and need relaxed environments, no matter where they are. They don't thrive under pressure. Just watch them eat dinner, and you'll see them taking their time, talking, and looking around, in no hurry. They tend to do most things slowly, and if they're chided to speed up, they can become nervous or even unglued or resentful.

Tend to your Harmonizer, and be sure they have what they need to thrive. That means a relaxed space and people to associate with. To be sure they do their homework and take care of their chores, simply tell them kindly and firmly what you expect and then hang around a little. Procrastination occurs in settings that don't support a child's energy and passion. Be supportive, guide them as they organize their bedroom, remind them to keep on task, and stay physically close by as they organize. Promise in a week or so (they aren't speed demons) their room will de-clutter and they'll feel proud! Harmonizers also come alive when their rooms are filled with more of a people presence, so decorate their desk and walls with photos of loved ones or memorabilia that conjure up good memories. These personal touches will make it easier for them to do their work and even get ready for school in the morning.

When it comes to getting a job done, Harmonizers are not big at initiating. They need more reminders to keep focused than most, but they will gladly wait to be told what is needed and will do their best. It is a challenge for them to be objective or analytical because, again, their thinking style is far more relational and collegial. Remember, their biggest fear is loss of social approval, so to get them motivated to tackle a big task, give them compliments ahead of time about how much they will please you and how their friends will love their well-organized room, and you'll see them get busy! When you validate them and give them a big hug for a job well done, they will have an easier time staying organized.

The Harmonizing child thrives in an environment that validates their feelings, devotion, and concern for everyone's well-being. The following list of adjectives describes the many facets of your Harmonizing-style child. They are not meant to pigeon-hole him or her into a limited set of definitions, but rather help to paint a bigger picture of your child's particular gifts and talents. Notice how you view these traits. Some might seem negative at first read, so take a moment and consider the positive side as well. For example, *dramatic* might be seen as "hysterical," or "little over top." Think again and you'll realize it also means "expressive" and "exciting." Knowing more about who your child is and how he or she ticks can inspire new ways to communicate and relate with your Harmonizer child.

Qualities and Traits of the Harmonizing-Style Child

- Adaptable
- Caring
- Cooperative
- Devoted
- Dramatic
- Emotional
- Empathetic
- Friendly

- Generous
- Intuitive
- Personable
- Sensitive
- Sociable
- Supportive
- Sympathetic
- Understanding

The Harmonizing child wants everyone to be happy! They are concerned about people and are sensitive enough to know when something isn't right. Getting organized can be tricky for them, but after you truly understand what matters to them and how they think, you'll find you'll be able to easily help them shape up their room, finish their homework, and enjoy life.

How the Harmonizer Relates to Time

> Success is like a vitamin. It is a vitamin deficiency to grow up success deprived.
>
> —Dr. Mel Levine, *Misunderstood Minds*

For most children, time moves slowly, but for the Harmonizer child, time crawls—five minutes can seem like an eternity. (Never mind them waiting for Christmas or another birthday to come around.) Harmonizers are motivated more by how they feel than the desire to produce something or achieve completion. Because they are more concerned with people than making quotas, traditional time management means very little to them. A phone call from a friend is always more important than their to-do list or a deadline. Naturally, this can sabotage a schedule, and consequently, Harmonizers are frequently tardy, often rushing around the very last minute to get things done.

The best routine for a Harmonizer is to organize their time into regular chunks, with frequent breaks factored in to allow them to connect with people. Although the interruptions might seem problematic to another thinking style, they help keep the

Harmonizer happy and more productive. Remember, doing any-thing alone is punishment for these social creatures. Again, they have a hard time staying on schedule and being punctual because they tend to choose an interpersonal activity over an impersonal task. They tend to get easily distracted by others. It's no surprise to hear their teacher or coaches sigh, "I can never find them!" You can help them out by convincing your Harmonizer that paying at-tention and getting things done on time makes a positive differ-ence to other people, including teachers, friends, and you!

In the morning, when you want to get your Harmonizer up and out the door, be sure you alert them about what needs to happen when. Let them know when they have ten minutes left to finish getting dressed. And help them start their day with a pleasant, noninvasive sound wake-up call. Find an alarm clock that announces the time with nature sounds. It will help them wake up without a start!

What the Harmonizing style really needs is personal "coaching" from parents and teachers. If you can help them set up their own calendar, decorated with pictures of pets and loved ones, including personal priorities and goals, your child may be-gin to learn how to take time for themselves instead of always running for others. This will help them learn how to become more balanced, energized, and ready to deal with the outside world. Another way to build an ongoing relationship with your child that teaches a better understanding of time is to ask them to cut out photos of family members and glue them on the appropri-ate date in the family organizer for a specific chore or activity.

Harmonizers tend to want to work with others. If they are working alone, it is important to coach them to understand how to connect with the subject matter of their report or essay. Building a relationship with learning is a great way to help the Harmonizer find purpose in things outside of socializing. If any project can connect them to what deeply matters for them, they can emerge victorious and feel like they have used less energy to accomplish their goals.

School can be stressful for them, and even though they get along with a variety people, they often miss out on important lessons due to being late or just not paying attention. Sometimes they are embarrassed and criticized for their seemingly lackadaisical manner. Again, if they can be reminded that being on time is a sign of caring for others, especially the teacher, this may help.

When it comes to their personal life, sometimes Harmonizers are overcommitted to every one and every cause. Being caught up in so many activities causes stress, and running here and there, from party to meeting to volleyball practice, can be exhausting. Remember, the primary purpose of your Harmonizer child is to love, feel appreciated, connected with others, and get social recognition. Naturally, they make a point of being part of everything and everybody. To help out, take charge of their after-school events and try to keep them to a reasonable number. It will provide them the quality time they need with you, the opportunity to rest and refresh for the next big bash, and an opportunity to keep life in balance.

The Harmonizer at Home

Your Harmonizer child enjoys working and playing by your side or with others. They need your help to get them going and keep them on track. You won't have to do everything, mind you, but your presence will create the socializing component that makes

> The physical, emotional, mental, and spiritual
> dimensions of being human are all connected;
> thus, attaining harmony with our physical en-
> vironment contributes to greater wholeness in
> our lives.
>
> —Sue Pearson, *Tools for Citizenship and Life*

them feel secure and motivated. This is a group effort, so get into the spirit! For example, you can pick up one thing and then they pick up another, and so on. They are happy to take any and all direction as long as you express your ideas in a voice that is tender. You might suggest an order for the stuff on their shelves—maybe big toys on the bottom, books on the next shelf and stuffed animals on top. You can also focus on the color, for example, saying pick up the blue things first, then red, and then yellow, etc. Again, remember, they won't want to do the organizing by themselves, so you be responsible for one shelf and they can do the next one. If they know they are needed, they will perform at top rate. Anything that nurtures their spirit of connectedness will help them want to stay and finish any work that needs to get done!

Harmonizers like to live in a warm, cozy, harmonious environment filled with plants, objects and pictures of places they want to go or have been, and photos of friends and family. This may appear cluttered to you, but chances are they like having a lot of things around them to feel secure and grounded. Of course, they tend to have way too much stuff. One of their biggest challenges is learning how to purge. They need a lot of structure and support when it comes to choosing what to keep and what to give away. This requires some real focus on your part, but the payoff is big. As you teach them that memories of experiences are as valuable as objects they seem to hoard, you'll be able to limit their collections. They also need to be informed that when they give stuff away, they are able to help other people and even save the planet by learning how to need less.

Giving things away is not easy for these children. Sometimes it is a good idea to get their friends together to help them when they clean out their closet. Maybe they can have a clothes-swapping party, but always monitor what you allow them to keep. If you turn your back, they'll probably be stuffing back into the closet all the dance costumes you both just decided it was time to give away! Instead of indulging them in boxes and boxes of memorabilia, it's great to create a few memory books. Help them make choices of photographs, and ask them to write a photo journal essay detailing your family's history over the past X number of years.

Harmonizers like to see what they have, so exposed shelving works great. Something like an over-the-door shoe bag for their Beanie Baby collection, costumes, or crafts can come in handy. Before you buy any nice new containers to hold all their stuff, sort out what you want them to keep and give away and then invest. It's best to avoid using homemade containers or egg cartons, say, for their art supplies. They just don't function well and fall apart quickly. Take your Harmonizer shopping for colorful containers, and when you bring them home, they'll love filling them up!

Harmonizers like to organize by type but also by color. Have fun organizing things together, and remember, if it is personal, friendly, vibrant, and colorful, they will enjoy using it and are more apt to return things and make it easier for you as well. Be sure their bedrooms are colorful as well. Their love of color is actually the key to successfully organizing these kids, so color-code their drawers and shelves to remind them where their clothes and toys go. Decorate their rooms with smiley stickers and colorful natural elements like feathers and pretty shells, and add a boom box that plays fun music and sounds from nature. These children usually like to help with the laundry, so get them a set of stackable plastic drawers to toss their dirty clothes in or put one in the laundry room just for them.

Make the place they do their homework comfy, warm, and nurturing with plants, vibrant colors, and photos galore. Be sure they have enough space. (A twenty-two-inch desk for a six-year-old and then a thirty-inch desk for someone entering junior high.) Make them an easy filing system so they can get in the habit of storing their tests and school accolades and future projects. Use different color hanging and interior files, and make attractive labels for each subject. They also enjoy using accordion files to store their treasured greeting and thank-you cards.

When it comes to their personal maintenance, Harmonizers tend to spend a lot of time getting ready and making sure things are just perfect. I had a client whose Harmonizer daughter had a collection of matching ribbons, one for every outfit. She was only seven years old but took the additional time in the morning to ensure that she looked just great! It's a challenge, but try to limit your Harmonizer daughter's clothes and hair accessories, or they will get out of hand!

Harmonizers tend to have a lot of things, and their personal space may be described as cluttered. When they arrive home, for example, they need a mini-mudroom area for their book bag, lunch box, and clothing. Give them a great basket or certain hooks for them to use. (You will need to remind them.) It's your job to keep this area streamlined and purged, but you will have less trouble inside their room if they get organized before they get comfortable in the house.

Harmonizers tend to want to help, so give them responsibilities. I recently had a mother/daughter organizing session, where once I taught the mother how to organize her own clothes, her daughter copied it and learned to maintain it herself. Provide them time to talk about the rules, and be sure they apply to everyone equally. Let them be the "Helper of the Day," and as a reward, they either get to pick out the video or choose what you'll make for dinner or even dessert! They would prefer not be in charge of tasks but rather be in the supporting role to you and your family. Because they like to nurture, have them take care of the pets. No matter what they do, small or grand, vocally show your appreciation and give them a hug.

Create rules for home space. It must be treated differently from their bedroom space. They need to be given "clean-up" time and aren't allowed to collect as much stuff, or leave it out in the open when it is a collective space. You may need to remind them about this, but in time, it will become a pattern and they will do it. They may whine and beg for what they want, and sometimes they will speak emotionally and ask more aggressively than they will act. Because their feelings play center stage and can take over what direction they are headed, if something doesn't go their way, you will know it for sure. They are usually the ones who are around the teacher the most or complaining a lot to their parents about what did or what did not happen at school.

Harmonizer children are not the best at taking disciplinary action. They prefer that someone else be in charge, so don't give them expectations that won't work out. They need to be told what to do, what is expected of them, and they will do it. They need someone to guide them and give them deadlines for things to be done. They enjoy helping out and really do value people and their thoughts. If you can inspire them to trust you, they will almost do anything for you. Harmonizers relate much better with those who need them and need to spend time with people who love them.

The Harmonizer at School

> The best training any parent can give a child is
> to train the child to train himself.
>
> —A. P. Gouthey

Counselors, therapists, teachers, healers, veterinarians, chaplains, chefs, and social workers are examples of occupations that serve people or animals. Your Harmonizing child may choose one of these. Because they have strong interpersonal skills and get along well with others, they enjoy socializing, have tons of friends, and may even feel comfortable in crowds. Harmonizers have an incredible sense of empathy and concern for others, so naturally schoolmates and friends come to them for advice. These children view school mainly as a social function, with their academic interests and pursuits coming in a distant second. Their aim isn't so much to learn, but rather to be appreciated and well liked.

Stimulated by school activities, especially performing arts such as drama, dance, music, and languages, they can contribute fun and optimism to the classroom while still respecting the teacher's authority. Some Harmonizers also like sports, especially because they understand the value of harmony when it comes to building a winning team. They are loyal to their teammates, gladly stepping out of the limelight for the group to come out ahead, and because they are total people-pleasers, they enjoy listening to their coach and doing whatever is asked.

When I lecture to CEOs, I sometimes mention how adult Harmonizers are often in charge of human resources at corporations across the nation. It makes perfect sense because they are sensitive to people's feelings and strive for harmony at home and at the workplace. If they feel compromised or in any state of conflict, they may internalize their pain. They don't want to make trouble and are terribly uncomfortable with any kind of conflict. Often Harmonizers hover close by their teacher when they are feeling extremely vulnerable.

It follows that Harmonizers aren't big on debate and even go so far as to trust other people's opinions over their own. They often avoid taking a position in an argument to avoid seeming unpleasant or confrontational and prefer to say as little as possible in fiery discussions. You may hear your Harmonizer child telling you things they think you want to hear, with some embellishments to boot, rather than make you unhappy. Because of their people-pleasing persona, they may hide how they feel.

Harmonizers can be shy when unsure of a situation and may become clingy when hurt or tired. Their teacher and classmates may also see them as a nonstop talker and a touchy-feely person. This can cause then to be disruptive in the classroom. Sometimes Harmonizers dislike school because they don't want to fail. Chances are, they will work for good grades to impress the teacher, but they may get only average ones because they're too busy socializing to study. They also tend to do what is asked of them and rarely think outside the box. Highly repetitive tasks or work that requires a lot of strenuous mental analysis can be difficult for them. Taking tests is a challenge, especially true/false or multiple choice tests. They are better suited to demonstrate a response. They like to learn by being in the middle of things, and activities that involve group sharing keep the Harmonizing-style child happy and productive.

When it comes to doing homework, they need to be around you when they are working. They may need help, and you may have to assist them in becoming and staying organized. Chances are, they may want music playing in the background or to get up and move around and then go back and sit down. But they will do their work; it just doesn't always look that way. Harmonizers like rituals. They need to do their homework in a special place. Be sure it has photos of loved ones hanging or on the desk and other attractive things. This is where they can sit down in comfort and think, "Time to get to work, but later I can be with my friends or family!" To ensure that things get done on time, be sure a calendar is right there next to them. Encourage them to use highlighters, colored pens, and markers to mark deadlines. Subdividing makes big tasks much easier for these children, so use full-colored index cards to help them divide their tasks, and have notebook dividers for all homework, school reports, and sign-in sheets. Set aside a special time to create some charts, covered with stickers and upbeat images, that illustrates their personal and academic goals. Chances are, they will do what is expected as long as it is colorfully spelled out and they have your regular encouragement and support.

One easy way to help them out is to be sure their school bag is packed every evening. Put a big list up, and be sure you check it so you don't forget things like parent's notes, lunch boxes, and personal items in the morning, and before they leave school, get them in the habit of checking their pocket list that lets them know what they need to bring home and back to school in the morning. For example:

- Lunch money
- Gym clothes
- Band instrument
- Permission slips
- School forms

- After-school activities
- Library books
- Special items
- Sports equipment

All in all, the Harmonizer child tends to do well in school, especially from a social position, and is seen as a success by many of their classmates. They enjoy having fun and making a difference in their school life and are always willing to be of service to their schoolmates, teachers, and coaches. School can be a challenge for them, as they tend to be afraid of really expressing themselves for fear of being rejected. Knowing this can help you encourage them to speak up, express what they feel, and not worry about being reprimanded or disappointing their teachers. Give organization a human connection, and you will likely be on the right track.

"The Dog" at Play

Playtime is especially fun time for Harmonizers. It means time to move freely, dance, talk, and connect with other kids. Harmonizers are certainly not interested in solo hobbies or quiet time alone. These active players are so much fun, always on the go. But they are also extremely accommodating to others, so be sure your

> Listen to the desires of your children. Encourage them and then give them the autonomy to make their own decision.
>
> —Denis Waitley, *www.stresslesscountry.com*

Harmonizer learns how to say "No" once in a while; otherwise they'll invite the entire third-grade class over for a slumber party on a weekly basis! A client's son recently had a birthday party and even though he initially was only going to invite a handful of his fourth-grade classmates, when he found out that the other students knew about his party and weren't invited, he invited the entire class! His mother, Angela, said that lucky for her she had a lot of extra pot stickers in the freezer!

Harmonizers love being busy! They are just as happy sewing, doing woodworking, or cooking as they are getting ready for a magic show or a dramatic reading. Playtime is their time to shine! This is a child who does well with an officially designated "activity center." Why not create one in a colorful corner in their bedroom? Try setting up a Reading Corner. How about a Theater Corner? Or maybe even a Dress-Up Corner?

These children are major collectors of memorabilia, from baseball cards to Beanie Babies. They really like to have all their favorite treasures around them at all times, and if no one is with them, they will spend endless hours creating conversations among American Girl dolls and their stuffed animals. Therefore, their toys and stuff are very important to them, but playing with their friends, dressing up, or just hanging out and having a playdate is good for them, too. Talking is very important to them, and families who fail to devote regular talk times at meals or after dinner may lose this Harmonizer to outside groups, where people are actively more engaged and available.

Make visual statements with their toys. You may even label the storage box on the outside. It is good to alternate their toys and have some out at certain times of the year and others out at different times. Toys that work for them could be stuffed animals, tapes related to people, board games, or cards. People-related toys are good for them and feed their soul. Make things fun and colorful, and they will be bound to put things back and feel accomplished.

Try to restrict toys to their room and family room, and keep their toys to a minimum. Restrict their environment, as that is any parent's first line of defense to minimize children clutter. Be a mindful shopper, and get things they need, or perhaps you can borrow things from the library or a personal friend. Also, you may limit their toys for special occasions or have your own reducing plan already in the works. Be consistent, as they tend to collect, collect, and collect memorabilia. Collecting meaningful things with good memories makes them feel grounded and supported.

The Harmonizing child likes to be busy with friends and has a lot of options for expressing themselves. What they do and what they possess are all about connecting. They are gatherers, and they need to get rid of things on a regular basis and find new meaningful homes for their things to go to. Give yourself time doing this with them; don't be rushed, as you may need to take a whole day to do it, or break it up into chunks. If that doesn't work, encourage them to have a minor sweep approach either one hour every Sunday or before they go to bed. Be sure you are present and encourage and support them doing this; otherwise, it may take a long while. Remember that they will be more wiling to give away things when they know where they are going.

Nurturing Your Harmonizing-Style Child

> So wherever I am, there's always Pooh, and me.
> "What would I do," I said to Pooh, "If it wasn't
> for you?" and Pooh said, "True! It isn't much fun
> for one, but two can stick together," says Pooh.
> "That's how it is," said Pooh.
>
> —A. A. Milne, *Winnie the Pooh*

The Harmonizing child likes spreading joy and good cheer along the way. They can be expressive and affectionate, and they deeply desire interpersonal connections. They like to give gifts as well as attention, and they are accommodating to the needs of others. They are generous with their time and with their spirit and are truly in service. Give them some time off, to hang out with their friends, where they can receive praises and acknowledgments on how giving and wonderful they truly are.

Find a mentor—every family has at least one member who is crazy about organizing—let them help the Harmonizing-style child get organized in a way that works for them. From their bedroom to the kitchen table, teach them responsibility by setting an example with what you do. They may want to flatter you by doing something the same way. Remember, it has to work for their brain; to maintain the system, it has to be fun and work for their friends, too! Here are some other fun ideas and practices you can put into place to make them feel good about themselves—which will motivate them to want to get organized and stay organized.

- Acknowledge their feelings.
- Give them "I" messages—"I get scared when I see you climbing on the bookcase because you might hurt yourself." Positive I messages really show them you care.
- Set up a "wall of fame" for all the good things they have done, especially when it comes to helping people.
- They need affirmation. It raises their self-esteem and helps children feel important. "I am so proud of you."
- Don't embarrass or reprimand them in front of other people.
- Give them personal assurances, support, and sincere appreciation. Show interest in them as people first, before you ask them to clean their room. "I really appreciate you and your enthusiasm and talents. I know you'll do a great job. Now, please straighten up your desk."
- Be open and candid. They'll know if you have a hidden agenda.
- Establish an environment of stability and security. Don't make any quick changes without preparing them first.
- Help them set goals, and give them rewards in words of praise and recognition.
- Help them make decisions and keep time commitments.
- Be less strict and more fun!

The Harmonizing child has a difficult time saying "no." They tend to put other people's wants and needs before their own. This is good news and bad news. They enjoy helping others and getting organized to be better of service and have things ready so they don't hold up the line. However, it is beneficial if they have some downtime and give back to themselves. Let them schedule it in, and comment to them how good it is to do just that.

Also, don't expect them to be the best on details or follow through, as they have a lot of items to keep track of and would rather be seen as being popular and kind than effective and efficient. Organizing for them has to be about connecting to people and things. So make yourself available to support them as they learn how to put their room in order, and you'll find yourself laughing, dancing, and talking along with them as they lift your spirits and pick up their clothes. With your help, the Harmonizing-style child can have a lot of success in getting organized in their own fun and harmonious way!

Harmonizing Style: "Dog" Overview

Purpose: To achieve harmony with people and things. Their surroundings need to be a bit more relaxed than the traditional definition of organizing, with easy maintenance systems in place.

Organization of space: Crave a relationship with people and their environment that is harmonious, peaceful, and comfortable.

Strengths: Sensitive and generous to the needs of others and passionate about wanting to be of service.

Challenges: Has way too many things and does not dedicate time to handling their stuff. Being on time and acting efficiently is a challenge. They are more concerned with feelings than productivity.

Harmonizing Style: Time

Calendar: Needs something that is motivating, so it's best to feature a photo of family/friends on the top of the calendar. Place it strategically, on their desk or bedroom wall. Personalize time for them. They can wear a fun watch or have a great alarm clock that plays sounds of the ocean. Anything to make time less objective and more inviting will do!

To-do list: It is effective if they can create one big list for each area, like homework, personal goals, or hobbies. Not a big list maker, like the Maintaining-style child.

Goals: All needs and motives revolve around relating to others. Help them organize their time to be sure they take care of their own work and play as well.

Strengths: Loves being with people, animals, or nature. Less concerned about time and more involved with engaging with others.

Challenges: Has a challenge sticking to a schedule when little help is provided.

Harmonizing Style: At Home

Bedroom: Enjoys a colorful, busy bedroom with lots of items scattered throughout. May have a lot of clothes, stuffed animals, plants, pets, fun pictures, or inspirational prints that make their space feel more alive and happy.

Closets: Does well sorting by style and color.

Drawers: Different drawers or stacking bins/baskets for different items by color and category. Not overly organized, but stacked horizontally.

Memorabilia: Needs to have a structure in place so they know how long to keep certain things and when to give them away. Need to keep as much stuff as possible with easy access.

Storage: The more attractive, the better. They'll have fun if things look pretty. Sometimes it helps to color-code their boxes.

Strengths: Enjoys helping others in performing tasks. Likes to keep a lot of special things around to remind them of happy times.

Challenges: Needs a friend or an organizing best buddy to help them determine what to keep and where to keep it.

Harmonizing Style: At School

Homework: Thrives in a comfortable environment, where people are around. Deadlines need to be set and enforced, kindly, by others.

Strengths: Social and helpful to their friends and kind to their teachers. Committed to working hard once they see how their work benefits or pleases others.

Challenges: Have a difficult time getting assignments in on time. Tend to spend time at school socializing more than studying.

Easy Ways to Get Your Harmonizer Child Organized

1. Be sure your Harmonizing child has an organizing buddy.
2. Be aware of how you ask the Harmonizer to do things. Modify your tone of voice, and be sure you sound and look friendly and fun.
3. Praise your Harmonizer regularly with compliments, applause, laughter, and even a (disposable) gift now and then!

4. They often like melody, tone, and rhythm. Having music in the background may encourage them to get organized, to do their homework, and have fun with friends.

5. They respond to color, which may invoke strong feelings. Color-coding their hangers—for example, white for casual, red for formal, etc.—will help them remember where things are located.

6. They thrive around their memorabilia collection. Displaying photos on their desk will motivate them to get their homework done. Even if the caregiver is busy around the home, they won't feel so lonely.

7. Don't store their memorabilia in the attic or garage; make it user friendly, and they will feel more nurtured and comfortable in their space.

8. They tend to remember faces or pictures. Use storage bins with photos on the outside, rather than a label.

9. Children are egocentric. They focus on their things, their room, their stuff, etc. Forcing them to purge their things can set up a lifetime of scarcity. Therefore, help them distinguish between need, want, or future wish list. Needs must be fulfilled, wants improve the enjoyment of life, and their wish list can be a big bonus.

10. When they are purging, it may be very difficult for them. Let them know where their stuff is going and perhaps even insist that they can give their things to people they know or take it to a recycling center themselves.

CHAPTER 4

Innovating Style:
"The Horse"

When I was in the fifth grade I had a wonderful
teacher who helped me believe in myself!
She taught me that my way of thinking was
not just different but special.
—Barbara Meister Vitale, *Unicorns Are Real*

Ethan was a wild child who lived large.
He could process varied and dense
information in no time flat and was
always involved in a hundred different projects all at the same time. (Yes, it's
true; Innovators are rarely masters of time
management.) Energized by problem-
solving, Ethan was a talented space planner, always rearranging his room with
endless solutions and millions of new
ideas.

His parents called me when Ethan was transferring from
middle school to a very demanding boarding school. They noticed that Ethan was getting everything done—just in the nick of
time—but were concerned he may be overwhelmed by his ever-
growing responsibilities. Together Ethan and I designed a colorful calendar with a new picture for each month. It kept him from

getting bored and in turn, could help keep all his activities and commitments straight.

When it comes to organizing success, the Innovating thinking style has the some unique challenges. They love freedom! Their unpredictability, like that of a wild horse, running freely with passion and zeal, truly tests the organizing gods. The Innovative child is so much like the horse. Both need freedom to move and explore, resist any kind of rigid rules or confinement, and crave to be independent and inventive. Horses roam from place to place, searching for open spaces, and are always on the go, looking for the next best thing. These qualities are not so easy to manage, especially in the mind and body of a child!

It's no wonder the horse is the magical hero of so much popular folklore. Horses conjure up a wondrous combination of qualities. Their strength and power ground them on this earth, but their beauty and grace lift them into the higher realms. Many ancient stories speak of the strong intuition and clairvoyance of the horse as they express their talents of divination. Similarly, the Innovating style combines magical inventive brilliance with charisma. Their zest for the new and unusual is what motivates and inspires them, as they go off galloping above the mundane humdrum of daily life.

Throughout history, the horse has helped build civilizations. Ancient cultures were built on the power of the horse, not only as transportation and a sign of beauty, but also as a sign of a country's wealth. Horses have stamina and great self-reliance. They are willing and able to carry heavy loads great distances. They work just as hard and intensely as the Innovating child, who knows no time boundaries and can work endlessly for specific periods of time if engaged in a unique project of passion and spirit. Big on adventure and discovery, both thrive in the realm of the unknown and unproven. The beauty of the wild horse has no equal, and they, like the Innovator, can uplift us from the mundane and help us transcend into more expansive realms of consciousness and creativity.

When it comes to getting organized, the Innovating child has a difficult time with predictability, uniformity, structure, and routine because it all seems confining, boring, and certainly no fun. Even though they initially are passionate about organizing and like starting and even setting up original organizing solutions, they aren't interested in maintaining them for long. If another organizing challenge confronts them, they may re-invent the wheel rather than do the same thing twice. Predictability isn't their preference, and they'd rather face a clutter nightmare than follow directions and put tab "A" into slot "B."

The horse and the Innovating style have the ability to persuade others to do what they want to see happen. They are also both confident and have appealing and persuasive abilities. But they need help being domesticated! Like the wild horse, Innovators will gallop in different directions simultaneously. They run here and there, always on the move, discovering new things and ways to implement them. When it comes to the actual upkeep, it doesn't really work. Who is going to slow down a wild horse to take care of the details?

Being on time is an even greater challenge for Ethan than it is for Alexis. No one—not his parents, teachers, or even friends—holds their breath when he is supposed to show up. Conventional solutions never worked for this Innovator. Even wearing a watch with an alarm or getting a phone call reminder vanishes into thin air as he slides into creative reverie. One day a solution hit him out of nowhere! Because he loves music and composing, he set up his keyboard with a timer and chose different pieces of music to play, like an alarm, for certain types of activities. School, lessons, and extra-special events all had their own songs attached to the timer! Luckily, his parents appreciated the music he picked out, and so did his siblings.

Ethan doesn't mind organizing—once a year that is! His parents are always after him to tidy up and put things away, but Ethan marches to the beat of his own drummer! His dad respects Ethan's individuality, so he came up with a fresh approach that honors this Innovator's innate needs and also the requirements of the household. Whenever anything new and exciting is about to happen—from family trips or another school year—Ethan is expected to organize his room and closet. Dad's solution really works because Ethan is motivated by new things up ahead and is more than willing to do his chores to get the reward! A chest of drawers doesn't work well. For Ethan, if it's out of sight, it's out of mind. His things are more likely to be stacked on top of the drawers than in the drawers.

School is challenging for Ethan. He certainly is bright enough, but the routine, details, and structure run counter to his nature. Because he seems distracted or is caught staring out the window, Ethan's teachers often place him in the front of the classroom to help him stay focused and more on task. Ethan was crabby about this special attention at first. "I don't want to be singled out!" he cried. Over time, his teachers and his parents helped him understand that his creativity and brilliance won't find expression unless he is supported by his instructors and encouraged to stay present, speak out, and follow through. Because he is passionate about some things but terribly disinterested in others, he has learned to allow the teachers to fuss over him a little so he can discover a more balanced and attentive rhythm in his work and play.

When Ethan is inspired, "watch out!" He is on it, and nothing stands in his way. He can be a tad bossy, even though he never means any harm. He is capable of playing by himself for hours on end. Ethan is never at a loss for creating new and exciting ways to create, discover, or imagine. He invents new games regularly and takes delight in inviting friends over to take part in one of his elaborate adventures.

Innovators are the opposite of the so-called ideal methodical, careful, everything-in-its-place organizer. Don't hold your breath; they never will be. When they want to get organized, they can blast into a somewhat impulsive blitz. They toss, throw, and dump almost everything they own; only to realize two weeks or three months later, they needed that volleyball. Then they throw their hands in the air, and you come in to help! Encourage them to solve their clutter issue, and they will. You don't need to enforce anything drastic, but you are needed to help this wonderful wild child put some systems into place to keep them safe and secure, so they are free to roam.

Innovators need as much freedom as possible. These children often have great ideas, so invite them to be part of your thinking process and make decisions together. Innovators love to lead, and with their strong vision and powerful minds, they are more than capable. Let them feel like they are in charge and then monitor them for accountability without them knowing it. It's really a win-win situation as you lovingly domesticate their wildness just a little into new and thrilling ways to get organized.

The Innovator's Thinking Style

> Rene crawled sadly back into bed. He stared at
> his ceiling. The ceiling was the only place in his
> room that wasn't messy. Rene wished that he
> lived on the neat ceiling instead of on the
> messy floor.
>
> —Julie Glass and Richard Walz,
> *The Fly on the Ceiling*

Chances are, your Innovating child may sound a lot like this: almost always late, assignments don't show up on time, challenged when there are more than two things to do in a row, not sitting at the desk working . . . sound familiar? You probably already know that when you approach this child with just the topic of organizing their room, they'll listen for a couple minutes, possibly try out one of your suggestions or invent their own, and then lose all interest. There are scientific inventions to birth and dance concerts to orchestrate! How do you approach these assertive children to make things work for them? First and foremost, keep it fun and keep it moving. These kids are very physical, and they learn the best when they are encouraged to move around. Give them some space, and they'll hop, skip, and problem-solve.

Organizing for the Innovating child also needs to be taught in a way that is amusing, creative, and playful with few rules or restrictions. It is all in how you communicate with them and how you approach the subject. Organizing can be made to be fun, and the Innovating child certainly has a lot of energy to get it all done; he just needs a nudge from you every now and then! Sometimes rewards work really well.

So how do you get started and guide them into a way to organize that actually works? Because the Innovator is the horse, you need to appeal to their passion, fierce energy, and physical prowess instead of their logical minds or desire to please. For example, make cleaning up their room a kind of game or sport. They like the big physical, dramatic moves, so encourage them to toss all the toys they don't want in a big plastic garbage bag and haul it away into the garage and load it into the car. When they get going, look out! Once on it, they can work with enormous vigor and stamina, and their body can go the extra mile, time and time again. Just keep stimulating and encouraging them, and you'll be amazed at how much they get done as they quickly and energetically gather, move, and purge! They will also grasp how good this feels when they are energized by the chore.

Innovators have a natural talent for spatial planning and abstract theoretical thinking, and they do have the skills to organize if they are interested! Because they are master problem-solvers, able to adapt to new situations, they are inspired to plan the next steps to, say, organize all the clothing in their closet. But they will often insist, with great certainty, that you should follow their lead and use their latest brilliant approach. Truth be told, their solutions will usually be stellar, but they may not be practical; they may be original, but not exactly easy to maintain. Now what to do? Be ready to rock 'n' roll when you start something with these kids. Their work drive isn't motivated by completion, but rather by discovering something new and unusual. Their work style is also either on or off, hot or cold. They tend to work in fits and starts. Therefore, break up the work sessions into several short time periods. Pay close attention to when they are in the mood to tackle clutter and then spirit them on to get it done.

Let them find their own unique organizing approach, where their passion to create and enjoy the process of getting organized reigns triumphant. Remember, they need the space to feel free and stimulated. Support their passion; encourage them to birth fresh, new organizing ideas; and trust that their enthusiasm alone will carry them and you along! Rather than nagging and hassling them with organizing strategies, arrange and create their space in a way that they can simply keep up and yet feel comfortable and nurtured by. They are not into maintenance, period. Create easy, straightforward solutions for them.

The Innovator child's thinking style is not well understood or appreciated. They tend to be taken less seriously than others, but ironically, in many ways, they contribute the most. They are the true-blue creatives, always contributing a new sense of vision, direction, or purpose, but like artists in general, they are often impetuous, illogical, (although not irrational), and difficult to control. The qualities of the Innovating child can be threatening because they upset the status quo. These strong-minded, powerful children thrive outside the box and may appear standoffish, rude, or even wacky. The following list of adjectives describes the many facets of your Innovating-style child. They are not meant to pigeonhole him or her into a limited set of definitions, but rather, will paint a bigger picture to enable you to open your eyes to many of your child's particular gifts and talents. Notice how you view these traits. Some might seem negative at first read, so take a moment and consider the positive side as well. For example, *assertive* might seem aggressive. Think again, and you'll realize it also means "self-confident" and "self-assured." Knowing more about who your child is and how they tick will inform and inspire new ways to communicate and relate with your Innovating child.

Qualities and Traits of the Innovating-Style Child

> With the aid of little saws, hammers, hatchets and tools of all sorts, Newton was constantly occupied during his play hours in the construction of models of known machines and amusing contrivances.
>
> —Catharine M. Cox, *Early Mental Traits of Three Hundred Geniuses*

- Artistic
- Assertive
- Charismatic
- Creative
- Curious
- Daring
- Imaginative
- Impulsive
- Independent
- Inquisitive
- Inspired
- Intuitive
- Inventive
- Spatial
- Spontaneous
- Visionary

The Innovating child seems to be the least motivated when it comes to everything, especially organizing. How they naturally do things is very contrary to how organizing principles are taught and maintained. However, they are also the most inventive and inspired of the thinking styles. Let's get started understanding more about this wild and wondrous "horse" and learn how to use their strength and passion to their benefit.

How the Innovator Relates to Time

> Children are apt to live up to what you believe
> of them.
>
> —Lady Bird Johnson, *www.stresslesscountry.com*

When it comes to time management, Innovators are truly challenged! They don't think about time the way many others do, chopped up into neatly manageable increments. To the Innovator, time doesn't really exist. They truly embody the notion of "be here now" and have little concern about the past or the future. However, when they are inspired by an idea or a task, they become incredibly committed and "Zen-ed" out. Time stands still, they fly into high gear, and nothing can stop them. They are either "on" or "off" when it comes to most things. Finding that passion and relating organizing to enhancing their creativity will go a long way.

The Innovating child usually prefers to be left alone with nothing planned, or they wish to set their own hours and schedule so they have plenty of time to think, create, and simply be. Your goal is to make time management fun for them, or at least make it easier for them to support their next creation and inventions! Their time management faux pas is in being chronically late much of the time because they are often caught up in the moment and simply forget. Don't take it personally. Rather, forgive them and practice instilling punctuality. They need ample notice and constant verbal reminders if they are auditory or pointing to pictures on a calendar if they are visual about what is about to happen and what time they need to leave by. Eventually, they will learn to know what is expected of them. Whether they choose to conform is another story!

To top it off, Innovators also like variety and have short attention spans for some projects. They are more prone to jumping up and out than sticking with a task and staying put. Like galloping horses, their thoughts and bodies run free. They are the visionaries and daydreamers. For them, time knows no boundaries. Unfortunately, because of this, many remain unfocused individuals who don't operate well in the "real" world, the one outside their heads. Naturally, others may view them as dilettantes or even loose cannons. They usually are not lazy, but definitely march to the beat of a very different drummer.

Innovators often work best when they do things the very last minute. They might request that you sew them a costume for tomorrow's recital or ask for money for next week's trip that was due two months ago! It is obvious they need your help. You may have to supervise them to ensure that things get done. Posting signs up in their room listing what is expected of them at school plus telling them verbally (over and over, yes) will eventually imprint the skills they need to be more successful within the realm of "traditional" life expectations. You might feel like you've failed, but persevere. It will pay off.

When it comes to school deadlines, Innovators aren't the best at estimating the amount of time it takes to finish that science project. This can be a tad frustrating because the Innovator child doesn't want to be watched or regimented but has the tendency to stay up very late to finish the assignment. If you can make tasks into games that have some fun and lots of humor, you're halfway there. Start with making some special daily or weekly calendars. Ask them to get involved and decorate it, especially highlighting the tasks and activities they've done well.

For school, create a pictured schedule for their notebook, including every term/week for special classes like music, PE, and art. Draw the symbol on the day they go to that class, and bring the schedule home so you will know when to bring special supplies, materials, or even clothing. Chances are the activities that most kids in this age category (seven to twelve) do during the week are:

- Make bed. Get rid of the spread and just use a quilt or duvet.
- Brush teeth/wash face.
- Get dressed.
- Eat breakfast.
- Feed family pet.
- Gather school stuff.
- Go to school.
- Leisure/lessons.
- Do homework.
- Eat dinner.
- Take bath/brush teeth.
- Pick up toys/clean up.
- Bedtime story.
- Lights out!

After-school activities may consist of:
- Eat snack.
- Play outside with friends.
- Do homework.
- Leisure—games, reading, art, hobbies.
- Cleanup. Chores.
- Eat dinner.

When creating a chart of these lists, be sure you encourage them to get involved. Have them check off what they've accomplished, and decorate the chart with stickers or stamps. By keeping them on schedule, you are now holding them accountable and ensuring their success. The more specific you are with what they should be doing, the better they will learn what is expected of them. If and when they deviate from the list or calendar (they will), they will be able to get back on a schedule because it is all spelled out right on the wall. They will eventually learn what works for them and get things done in their own order and in their own time.

When it comes to returning things from the library or friends, try to have a mudroom, a kind of dedicated welcome-home-and-leave-home pit, where they can drop their book bags and lunch boxes without much fuss. This eliminates piles of stuff on the kitchen table or in the car and keeps important school/play items close to the front door. Yes, this is your assignment. If you don't have this kind of transition room, make some space, even a big container in a corner of the room.

Like the teachers do at school, give your Innovator a warning notice, maybe five minutes before cleanup time. You can wander in the living room and tell them, "Five minutes and then toys are put away." (Why make them put toys away in their own bedroom? Only in general living areas should the traditional organizing approach come into play.) Come back in three minutes and repeat. You will get a little exercise out of this, and they will eventually become attuned to getting something done on time. Also, set the kitchen timer for five minutes when you make your first announcement. It's a great tool because your child can hear it and you won't have to turn it off. Keep this simple routine steady and in place (they will want to change the rules, use a different timer, you name it) and they will try or get angry!

You must be firm and direct with your requests. Try not to talk down to them, and don't be critical or they will instantly pull back and resist. And please don't overschedule them. Actually, for them, a schedule is a mini-prison, and they'll get quickly overwhelmed and depleted. Limit their extracurricular activities, unless they are extroverted and chances are they may even need more activities, and you will have a much easier time at home. Here are two very important things for you, the Innovating parent, to practice: be consistent, and be specific.

Be very thoughtful about rules. Focus on a few important ones, and be consistent about adhering to them. Be sure you also eliminate unnecessary distractions, and give them sufficient time to complete all their tasks, from school assignments to house chores. They love "new"! These kids often like multiple activities and projects. Give them variety by moving from one to another. The Innovating child likes to be kept busy, thinking, and working. When you share a big-picture image of what is happening as you put organizing systems in place, they will understand that their part is important and will channel their inventive enthusiasm to the tasks at hand.

"The Horse" at Home

Your Innovating child not only has a hard time keeping track of time, but also is challenged with keeping track of their things. These days, most kids have so much stuff, and their lives are heavy with activities and hobbies, but the Innovator leads the pack with multiple interests and piles of . . . well . . . you name it.

Sweaters, crayons, books and balls, cars, and
puppets, paper dolls/pictures, papers, dogs
and blocks, Teddy bears, and dirty socks/
pencils, boxes, bows and lace, not one thing
was put in place.

—Elise Peterson, *Tracy's Mess*

These children are very unique, and so are their organizing cy-
cles. They collect a ton of art supplies, CDs, batteries, and books,
and then one day, seemingly out of nowhere, they spontaneously
purge. Before you know it, almost everything is gone, until the cy-
cle begins again. This is usually the way it is. Don't worry though;
they will clutter and declutter in their own way and in their own
time. When you want to get involved with your Innovator's organizing, think store it, donate it, or throw it away. They do well
tossing the stuff they choose to keep into large colorful baskets or
bins. That might be as far as they go in their organizing frenzy,
but at least clothes and toys can be cleaned up easily.

Of the four thinking styles, Innovators tend to be the most
inventive and unpredictable. That is why they need more room,
more space, more flat surfaces, and more freedom than the other
three styles. Their deep-seated curiosity about almost everything
requires lots of room so they can explore and move. They are also
true blue originals and may dress in "original" ways. Twelve-
year-old Vivian, for example, enjoys wearing her swimming gog-
gles to school! Tommy, an eight-year-old, prefers sporting different
colored socks and a bow tie. Both sets of parents used to scold
their kids for being too unconventional. Over time, they've
learned to respect and delight in their Innovator's "quirks" and

appreciate their desire to explore novelty, without wreaking too much havoc!

Here are two tools that will help your Innovator when it comes to success in organizing. First, be sure they have most of their things out in the open. Obtain stacking wire baskets so items, including clothing, can be off the floor and still "seen." If it's out of sight, it's out of mind for these children. Set up large, open shelves or big tables and let them spread out their toys, games, and books. Second, simplify everything. How? Don't buy them so much stuff. Make it easy on them and limit their wardrobe and collections of things. Also, make routine activities faster by buying Velcro closures on shoes and zippers on shirts instead of buttons.

When it comes to clothing, always go for comfort over style. You might even put their outfits together for them ahead of time so they don't have to think about what to wear and what not to wear. However, they may not want to be told how to dress and do want to mix and match on impulse. It is great if you can separate their clothing into categories, like clothes for school, play, or dance, all hung up together in their closet. Then they can simply leap into the closet, pull out something, and be "outta there" in no time. You can paint the closet rod (for clothing that is hung up) in different colors to section out the school clothing from play or formal wear. Don't get a dresser with drawers. They'll be half open and contents will be spilling out. Create space and buy less, and your Innovator's environment will be easier for them to manage with more room for them to explore and enjoy.

For example, Rachel is a competent and loving mother and wife. She has three children under the age of six but still manages to work part-time. While organizing her pantry, she mentioned she felt inadequate as a parent because her eldest daughter's room was such a mess, cluttered with books, dress-up clothes, and toys. She took the quiz and discovered that Lily's brain prefers an Innovating style. She is a creative, energetic, and humorous child who is always on the go. Rachel didn't know what to do with Lily, whose organizing preferences certainly didn't match her own Harmonizing style. (Rachel found out her own brain type, too!)

One great way to provide guidance and order for an innovator is to install as many hooks as possible on the walls of her room. Lily likes to move freely and quickly. Putting stuff into drawers makes no sense for her, because if it's out of sight, it's out of mind, but picking things up and hanging them on hooks is actually fun and easy. It supports her love of movement without restriction. Another idea that appeals to the Innovating style is putting a collection of big, colorful catchall bins in the corners of the room. Again, this solution encourages neatness without cramping their natural style. Lily's mother learned that making things overly complicated or too meticulous would spell defeat instead of victory for her child.

Another area of challenge for your Innovator is self-care. They just don't like to take the time to fuss over brushing their teeth or hair, clipping their nails, or bothering whether their clothes even match. Who wants to be burdened by mundane chores when they are inventing a new kind of airplane or remodeling their future home in their mind's eye? Don't forget, these children are also impulsive. They may floss their teeth three times a day and then suddenly, for no known reason, stop altogether. Unfortunately, to keep up their hygiene, you'll have to show up regularly to remind them to do this and that. Try for at least once a day!

Organizing is a roller-coaster experience for the Innovator, who may really enjoy it initially but then struggle to keep up. One easy way to help out is to buy a bunch of colorful fun clocks. Put them everywhere—in the bathroom, bedroom, and playroom, and on their desk, and on their wrist. That way they'll sense that time does exist. Another way to help them have fun organizing is to make colorful paper wheels featuring all the house chores, along with a spinner in the middle. (Or have a jar filled with colorful pieces of paper of household to-dos.) Let the Innovator run the activity like a game, where everyone closes his or her eyes, reaches in, and randomly chooses the chore of the day. Keep it fun and uplifting, and chances are they will be glad to do it.

Innovators need a lot of help getting organized for their studies. Start by creating an atmosphere that makes things fun, favorable, and a friendly environment. How? Color is a great solution. Use different color file folders for different subjects, and don't file them away into a drawer but put their collection of folders right on their desk. You may also want to have a set of books at home and a set of books at school so they don't forget them. If you can give them the room and space to create, really examine what they need to be creative, and ensure that no one bothers them, they will be grateful.

All in all, homework time can be rough on parents if their Innovator-style child's homework isn't in good order or systems are not put into place. Homework becomes more and more about organization as the child gets older and progresses through the grades. It is hard for them to keep track of things, especially when they change schools or grades and have different classes and new classrooms. It is a good idea to keep a list of numbers of friends or responsible classmates to call to find out about what the homework assignments are. The Innovator won't file and will forget labels that were put on file folders. Therefore, try to make it an activity that they enjoy doing. Buy them fun yet user-friendly crates, and create categories such as ideas, summer camp, and school classes. Have a wire basket on their desk dedicated to homework only. Have a hook on the wall where only their backpack is hung.

How can they keep track of what each teacher wants done every night and assignments that need to be handed in the next day? You may suggest a list, but certainly do not ask them to write down their homework for every subject, every single day. They would never keep that up, and it would be stressful for them. Instead, give them a homework planner that has a lot of room and plenty of space to write in. They may have two columns; one for the assignment and the second column for what supplies are needed for the project. They may need your assistance to track the due date of longer-term assignments and upcoming tests. It is best that you ask them when they come home and also make them do their homework before dinner and try to minimize distractions.

At the end of the homework time, check their homework book, making sure they completed everything and examine what is coming up ahead. Lastly, regarding homework, create a special place they can put it and easily retrieve it before school. Give them the same place, the same time each day to do their homework. Getting started is the hardest part for them, so sit with them, coach them, and let them be on their way. Let them only focus on what the next step is and try not to get let lost in the clouds.

Repetition for them is the real deal-breaker! They are best at starting something and need a great deal of encouragement for most routines. Perhaps a timer to be set goes off when they are supposed to be done their homework and washing their hands before dinner. Or using music to inspire them, every song to be choreographed to a certain organizing task. For example, one song is used to pick up clothing, another song is used to organize their bookcase, and so on. Give them limits and some loose but structured time. Also, let them put on their 'homework t-shirt' to set boundaries of what is expected of them.

Make the distinction between public and private areas of the home. Alert them to the different standards each room has. They hate rules, so don't use the word if possible. Keep clutter out of common living spaces, but let them feel relaxed in their own room. Because they are stackers and need things to be in sight as much as possible, their supplies could consist of:

• Tall stacking wire grid boxes/baskets for miscellaneous supplies and materials.
• Clear plastic boxes so they can see items inside.
• Desk for pencils, paper, and writing supplies.
• Bookshelves for books, puzzles, and equipment.
• Magnetic boards where art could come and go and they would be happy to have it up.

When you want them to organize their bedroom, never say, "Go clean your room." Rather, be specific; focus on the actual space or the actual subject. For example, say, "Pick up everything off the floor," or "Place your books on the bookshelf." Whether you get them in a system for everyday maintenance and then a more thorough system on the weekend, like Sunday night, before school, they will figure out the pattern. Let them create their own organizing categories, which they can change up from time to time, depending on their mood and energy level.

Lastly, they need support and encouragement for their choices and for you to make things safe for them to explore in. These kids really need your support and help getting things set up because they really can't do it by themselves. I would say that half of the children I work with are Innovating children, whose organizing style is very different from that of others. Don't go over the top with schedules, planning, to-do lists, and so on. If you want them to have that obvious structure, let them design their own forms, school checklist sheets, and the like. They need freedom as much as possible in their own space, because the culture requires them to conform to so many rules in the outside world. Face it: they may never be as organized as you would like, so don't nitpick the results.

The Innovator at School

> If I had one wish for my children, it would be
> that each of them would reach for goals that
> have meaning for them as individuals.
>
> —Lillian Carter, *www.stresslesscountry.com*

Out of the four thinking styles, the Innovators are typically the most curious and contemplative. Unfortunately, schools tend to support the conventional. Therefore, often Innovators feel terribly confined inside the restrictive educational structure. Although Innovators have the ability, they might perform poorly in their classes, again because they don't have the freedom they need to be creative and expressive. They would much rather immerse themselves into a task and finish when they feel they are done than start and stop classes, on someone else's schedule, again and again. They may find themselves loving certain classes like art, design, or the study of other cultures (anthropology) and find other classes hugely boring. Because they are quickly bored with routine tasks and restless when it comes to the minutia of things, they might act out when pressured to focus on details.

Their main skills are problem-solving, inventing, initiating, and discovering new ways to think and create. They have a creative nature and even may have some elements of "genius" thrown into the mix. Chances are, they excel in geometry and space planning, science, or music and the arts. They are also comfortable in the realm of ideas and might become the great motivational speaker, one who inspires people to think outside the box. It is interesting to note that most of their great ideas or novel approaches seldom come from sitting down at their desk. They like to move and do new things and, therefore, are able to create room in their mind that lets them imagine something else.

In school, Innovators will test the limits and appear fearless. When they take a test, they prefer essay style, where there isn't one "right" answer and they are encouraged to express themselves. They often have great ideas, but they may find writing it down too difficult. They may finish an exam five minutes after they get the paper or linger on the first sentence until the bell rings to end the session. They need an incubation time to get their minds and head around an idea, but once they get it, they can multitask like crazy and can get more done in a half an hour than most can in a day.

It is best if your Innovator can sit in the front of the classroom with his or her back to other students. That will help them focus and not be distracted by everyone around them. There are a number of ways teachers can help them at school, and parents can even use some of these approaches at home:

• Post rules on the board.
• Post the schedule on the board.
• Present new instructions, one at a time, making sure they are clear and concise.
• Put a homework basket in a visible area.
• Have them date their homework and be sure their name is on all assignments.
• Provide a quiet area in the classroom for them.
• Give both oral and written tests, if possible.
• Always ask if they have any questions.

Innovators tend to remember images, create spatial sequences, solve three-dimensional puzzles, and foresee existing or future patterns. Because they like to work with shapes and building blocks, they continually create structures that allow for new patterns to emerge. Innovators also can move at the speed of light when discovering something. They can also get bored easily and need more stimulation or a change of scenery. They have a hard time sitting still for a long period of time and really need to be passionate about a project to stay put at it.

They tend to be open to new possibilities and like a variety of classes and hobbies at school. On the other hand, they have a hard time with small, patterned motor sequences, like writing and using small objects. These are not meticulous children unless they are interested in the topic. Chances are, they are not the best spellers, and their handwriting might be less than legible. They may read ten books at the same time yet never finish one or jump around in the books.

While they often have very high standards, they may have a difficult time with follow-through on the little details and elements. Give them a huge bulletin board or dry-erase board that they can use to collect information, know where deadlines are, and hold people's contact info. They would benefit from seeing it out and in front of them. That is less work for you, to keep reminding them about their lessons or what they need to bring to school. They often excel using a computer once they are over the initial learning curve.

If they are allowed to explore new possibilities and create and imagine new ways to expand their experiences, they will be able to express their creativity and might develop some amazing skills. Their expressiveness and expansiveness are qualities that are often highly valued later in life but are not easily supported or even encouraged in a traditional school structure. Here are some tangible ways you can support them in school and at home:

- Provide an area where they can create their own homework area.
- Don't confuse or distract them from their studies.
- Let them know that it is human to make mistakes.
- Give them challenges, stimulation, and choices.

Teachers are only responsible for about 15 percent of your child's education; the rest is up to you. Keeping them on time and organized with homework and chores will help them feel more comfortable and secure and will ultimately provide the base for their many brilliant creative and intellectual leaps. They need help, understanding, and compassion to be organized.

"The Horse" at Play

> One of the advantages of being disorderly is that one is constantly making exciting discoveries.
>
> —A. A. Milne, *Winnie the Pooh*

The Innovator's inner world is very alive and bright! They like to draw and play games with strong visual and spatial aspects. They are often adept at puzzles and mazes. They may enjoy their own activity center where they can hang out to dream, doodle, or map out a new idea. Give them a comfortable corner to read books (introverted) that are heavily illustrated, and be sure there are open shelves with lots of art supplies so they can color in cartoons or make up a new story.

If they aren't completely engrossed in an activity, chances are they want to be running around outside, playing hide-and-seek, or simply exploring the back forty. They usually like individual sports (if they are sports-minded). Some enjoy playing chess, especially if they lean toward introversion. Of course, in the middle of reading, drawing, or running, these Innovators might suddenly switch gears and do something completely different. Surprises abound, 24/7.

When your Innovator discovers their next passion, they will rush in like there is no tomorrow. They will read every book in sight and will become the resident expert, seemingly overnight! They have this incredible ability to absorb information and understanding on an intuitive level. Because life is such a wild rush, filled with a huge amount of daring and energy, they might find it difficult to understand kids who are different from them. Sometimes, they may even offend their friends but won't know it. Innovators tend to be involved in their own world, and so they may fail to listen to others, ignore rules, or even make up new ones when playing a game. Other kids might find this upsetting. The Innovator dislikes conflict and tends to distance him- or herself both emotionally and physically. Because they are spontaneous, they may change direction suddenly, and it's not always easy to convince others to follow suit. They may not mind whether anyone else follows.

Because they are charismatic and like to have a good time, they attract friends. But they like to play practical jokes, have mega-active fun, and don't want to be around anyone who is dull or bosses them around. They have a good sense of humor and can be good leaders, as they are great at birthing a new project, but they may have less tenacity or follow-through for projects or friends. They are spontaneous, so they tend to welcome change, new faces, and new activities. They tend to approach life with a sense of joy and wonder, and because they don't take things too seriously, they enjoy joking around and making others laugh.

Play gives the Innovator the space and time to thrive and

actually replenishes their energy. They do not want scheduled playdates and prefer organically moving from this and that as the interests call them. Their creativity truly comes to light when they are at play, so be ready to be the audience and sit back to soak in a hundred or more piano concerts, dancing extravaganzas, or speeches on the future of the rocket ship.

Nurturing Your Innovating-Style Child

> Hide not your talents, they for us were made.
> What's a sundial in the shade?
> —Ben Franklin, *www.brainyquote.com*

Innovators are imaginative and independent souls. If you as a parent have a different thinking style from your child, it may be a challenge to parent a child who seems so daring and yet self-contained. Just think about how you feel when you watch them engrossed in a project, so absorbed, maybe for hours. You worry. You can't believe they don't come up for air. You wonder if they are okay. And you can't believe they don't need your help. You wonder how they came up with such a remarkable drawing, story, or novel invention. Along with their originality and remarkable vision, they are still innately disorganized according to traditional standards. They may be late for dinner. Their room may look like a tornado hit it. Again, don't worry. Your Innovator will get organized, but on their own terms and when they are in the mood. By the way, a word of warning: don't move their stacks! They won't like it! Ah. The challenges as a parent are real, but so are the rewards.

The Innovating child tends to be flooded by ideas and can become overwhelmed. Chances are, this child's approach to life mirrors Annie Dillard's wonderful description, "You've got to jump off cliffs all the time and build your wings on the way down." Because they tend to feel more in process and less organized than most, they need you to create external organization in your home. Routines aren't their style, but some structure can help them feel more secure. Be sure their homework schedules are in place and up to date, always have a morning to-do list and a bedroom checklist, and let them know what chores you expect them to do on a daily basis. Having these reminders out and up will greatly reduce the number of times you have to tell them what to do, help you keep your voice in check (no need to yell again and again), and prevent resentment on their part. No matter what, always give your Innovator the choice about how they want to do things. You can support them by breaking big tasks into smaller steps.

Unfortunately, friends and teachers do not always see Innovators in a positive light. They tend to describe them as unpredictable, not entirely dependable, a bit impulsive, or a disruptive force rather than a supportive team player. They generally refuse to plan too far in advance, and when engaged in a group effort, from a party to a sporting activity, they are filled with zest but may fail to pay attention to the particulars. Doing repetitive things, from practicing a musical instrument to making sure all the t's are crossed and the i's are dotted on a party invitation can be a challenge. They can choose to do so, however!

Innovators like having their own space. Give them their physical and mental room to move and think, and they'll fly. Innovators are just that—innovative. They are the entrepreneurs, risk-takers, writers, artists, and explorers. When their home atmosphere encourages them to be expansive and to daydream, not only will they do great things, but also they'll develop the kind of confidence and self-esteem required to really build a foundation underneath their big ideas. What could be better?

Rules and structure aren't something Innovators really respect, but they need some limits. It will take time to establish bedtime routines or homework times, but try to convince them that some routines can actually open up more time for exploration and adventure. They are rule-breakers. Explain why a few basic rules are necessary for you and the family unit, and expect them to try to honor them. Bottom line advice: give your Innovators advice, not orders, and operate from agreements rather than assumptions. They are avid seekers of knowledge and new approaches. If you couch your "rules" as new ways to do things, they may get curious and follow through just for the sake of a good experiment. Whatever it takes!

Less is more for the Innovator child once you decide on the chores and responsibilities (e.g., daily, weekly, monthly) and then decide what the actual chore is all about. If you can let them select their own style, for example, playing "beat the clock" to their own song, they are more likely to be successful. If their style still bothers you, just go with it. Organizing isn't about being inflexible or hypervigilant and neurotic. It is about establishing some structure to help guide and nurture the Innovating style and keep their life as simple and efficient as possible.

Innovating Style: Overview

Purpose: To be creative, expand their horizons, notice new things and patterns, and cultivate a vision of the future.

Organization of space: They need to have things out in the open as much as possible. They keep track of things they can see.

Strengths: They are very creative, quick workers, and when they want to accomplish something, they do it with great passion and force. They are great at originating ideas. They are big-picture thinkers.

Challenges: They have a hard time with follow-through and completion of details. They do not like to be told what to do and how to do it.

Innovating Style: Time

Calendar: If it is big and strategically placed, they may use it. May need some support with follow-through.

To-do list: Don't even attempt it!

Goals: Able to originate many new ideas in very little time.

Strengths: Are hyperfocused when they are working on something they enjoy or are interested in. If inspired, they make the most of every moment.

Challenges: Need to be reminded when things are due and of appointments that need to be met. Do not like to be disturbed by others.

Innovating Style: At Home

Bedroom: Prefers that personal belongings be left out. Need hooks for clothing and nets hung here and there to hold stuffed animals, toys, etc.

Closets: Find it much easier to hang rather than fold because they are better able to see what's there and it is easier for them to remember to use it.

Drawers: Get rid of them! Use clear plastic or wire grid stacking boxes.

Memorabilia: Tend to keep some of it, for no apparent reason, and then out of the blue, will toss it out and not look back.

Storage: Visually store things in clear boxes with lids or wire systems so they can be stacked and seen. Make this as easy as possible.

Strengths: Are good at space planning and organizing things in unique and personal ways.

Challenges: They may need help purging annually and getting things organized consistently. They like to be left to their own devices much of the time.

Innovating Style: At School

Homework: Need your help to get things done with the right materials, books, and files and handed in on time. May need to have two sets of schools books and have a homework notebook that has in one column, a date for what is due, and what it is, and another column listing the supplies.

Strength: Are very creative and an inspiration to their classmates. Are funny and able to come up with original and uplifting ideas.

Challenges: Tend to do things at the last minute and can lose important papers and materials. Also, they tend to think about projects ahead of time and then actually do them at the last minute.

Easy Ways to Help Your Innovator Child Get Organized

- Don't move their things (if you can help it!). Remember that they need their stuff left out so they can see it.
- Purchase furniture that works! Antique dressers that are hard to open and close or a hanging rod in their closet that is too high will not work. Make it easy for them.
- Get clothing out of dressers, and buy clear, plastic, or wire stackable containers and install hooks for their things.
- Give them a fifteen-minute warning when it comes to leaving the house. They need wrap-up time or get-ready time.
- They may tend to forget names or labels. Placing the item that is stored in a container on the outside of the storage box may be easier and more fun for them.
- They often have strong intuitive or gut feelings about where things should go and be placed. Let them assist you, and they will feel like they are contributing to the cause of organizing.
- They tend to act impulsively, and when it comes time for them to want to get organized, try to have extra supplies available, so when they are in the mood, you are ready!
- They communicate using gestures, so create space for them to get organized. If they are organizing their homework binder

and have limited space on the desk in their bedroom, allow them to use the dining room table.

- Motivating them to get organized, more often initiated by you rather than them, must be seen by them as an adventure. Make it fun, new, and appealing, and because they are hard workers, they will work with you until it is done.
- Remind them that they always give up something to get something. If they like keeping things, then they will have less space, less room for other things.

CHAPTER 5

Prioritizing Style:
"The Lion"

> It is evident that there are two leading factors
> in producing a man and making him what he
> is: one the endowment given at birth, the
> other the environment into which he comes.
> —Catharine M. Cox, *Early Mental Traits
> of Three Hundred Geniuses*

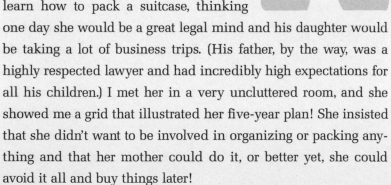

Jane was a very able girl who delegated every duty she thought was "beneath" her. She had no desire to perform tasks that were not related to her pursuit of personal and academic goals. Working up to the last minute in a whirlwind, she was packing for her eighth-grade summer trip to Italy. Her father wanted her to learn how to pack a suitcase, thinking one day she would be a great legal mind and his daughter would be taking a lot of business trips. (His father, by the way, was a highly respected lawyer and had incredibly high expectations for all his children.) I met her in a very uncluttered room, and she showed me a grid that illustrated her five-year plan! She insisted that she didn't want to be involved in organizing or packing anything and that her mother could do it, or better yet, she could avoid it all and buy things later!

I demonstrated that she could have her suitcase packed in fifteen minutes flat. I packed matching outfits so she could take the bare minimum and even challenged her to tackle doing it herself in less than ten minutes. Motivating a Prioritizer to save time and be more efficient is what really resonates. Her parents later told me she could now pack a suitcase in under five minutes. A Prioritizer will often want to take a challenge and take it one step further!

Who is the king of the jungle? Your Prioritizer child, that's who! This child likes to be in the position of authority and power and be in charge. Just take a look at the dignified gait of your strong-willed child. Do you see a CEO of a CFO in training? No doubt. These kids have the drive and determination to tackle any task that fits in with their goals and are willing to work, nonstop, to successfully complete it. Because they have such strong personalities, the minutia of the mundane doesn't sit too well with them. Because they focus on the big picture and not details, they excel in leadership, power, and strength. You may not want to get in their way. They are serious taskmasters; love to take charge and delegate; and even at a young age, are determined to do whatever it takes to become a success.

The charming Prioritizing child has many of the same qualities of the lion. Both have strength, zest, and confidence and are rarely intimidated. Being at the top of their class or roaming the savanna, they exude confidence and charisma. Throughout history, the lion has been the symbol of power. Being the second-largest cat in the animal world, the lion is mighty indeed and can run eighty kilometers per hour. With one well-orchestrated hit, it can take down a zebra or horse without missing a beat. It's no surprise almost all animals and people will back away when they spot a lion—or Prioritizer—nearby!

The Prioritizing child may not have the best social skills and may intimate people or dismiss them without really knowing who they are. They tend not to take things too personally and show little signs of emotional connection when they are confronted. Because they are always seeing the finish line and wanting to get to their next level, they look past people's feeling and believe that they need to be in control and dominate the situation.

Like the lion, the Prioritizer likes to show off their power by roaring loudly as they tackle their next big challenge. Always on the prowl to claim dominance over everybody and everything, both are hungry to achieve their goals. They may not tell you they mean business, but just by their presence, you know it. On the other hand, it is interesting to note that lions and Prioritizers tend to be hugely loyal to their families, and as long as they are seen as the center of attention, they will do anything to ensure that people are taken care of.

Sometimes the lion and the Prioritizer appear to be calm and silent. Don't be fooled; they are always living like they own the world. Hidden behind their regal appearance is a powerhouse of fierce determination and a dynamite focus. When the time comes for them to leap, they will. They want things done on their terms and may have no qualms about putting the fear of God into anyone and everyone who gets in their way.

Jane likes to keep her valuable time all to herself. She takes pleasure in completing her projects and can't bear to waste time. In the eighth grade, she understands that she prefers others to do things she's not interested in. But delegating all the household duties to her mother hasn't gone over that well! Jane's mom knows her daughter likes being a leader, and rather than fight City Hall, she decided to engage Jane in the tasks at hand. She had her daughter write down all her household duties and then asked her to pick out one to do for each day of the week. Naturally, Jane chose the ones that required the least amount of time and eventually combined them all into one wild blitz day. Her mother agreed because it got the job done. Jane is a master time manager, even at a very young age.

At home, Jane really doesn't like sharing her stuff, period. Her room is her castle, and she refuses to allow anyone, particularly her siblings, to borrow, use, or even touch a thing unless she gives them permission. Jane even wrote up a document she had her little sister sign that guaranteed she wouldn't break or ruin anything, any time, any place! This Prioritizer certainly understands boundaries, even to the point of the ridiculous. When she demanded that her parents put a lock on her door for her things to be protected, they said no. One day Jane will make sure everything works the way she wants. She'll just have to grow up first!

At school, Jane usually gets straight As. Jane has a goal to graduate as soon as possible and is very focused on attaining that goal. Jane often underachieves, rather than thrives, in the school environment and only has her mind on one goal, the goal of graduating. She wants to do well, but she often does the minimum amount of work necessary so that she can spend time pursuing her own goals and achievements. Sometimes she even feels she knows more than her teachers. When it comes to exam time, Jane has all her notes in perfect order and even makes charts and graphs to help her remember the facts. Nothing comes between this girl and her challenge to shine!

At play, Jane likes to play hard and tough with friends. She is the best at playing tag, hide-and-seek, and dodge ball. Intimidation is her strongest characteristic, and she is determined to win at all costs. Because she is so confident, she usually becomes the captain and everyone wants to be on her team. Although she can be intimidating, her friends really look up to her, knowing that they are in good hands and will probably beat everyone else on their roster. Let's face it: if Jane were selling lemonade on the corner, she would make more money than most—and have the best-quality lemonade.

The Prioritizer tends to be careful about how they spend their energy and save it up for the big tasks at hand. Organizing is something the Prioritizer plunges into headfirst if and when they believe it is necessary and important. They will prefer to delegate the details, however. If you need someone to take charge of organizing the entire house and garden, look to the Prioritizer. Of course, they won't want to be bothered with the details, but they'll happily call the shots, keep everyone involved and on track, and make sure the job gets done—and done well. Hey, it's their kingdom! Just be sure you are willing to give them the stage, and they'll make it happen.

The Prioritizer's Thinking Style

The wisest have the most authority.

—Plato, *www.brainyquote.com*

If you are able to provide the Prioritizing-style child with the right guidance and inspiration, you will have a great ally by your side. They love learning, and they absorb information best when it is given to them in distinct, logical, factual packets. Brief and to the point is the ticket. Don't try to entertain them, talk down to them, or restrain them, or they will get angry and refuse to listen. But when you present new material in math or requests to clean up the garage in a clear, objective, and straightforward manner, you'll be amazed. They'll get it, and they'll do it. Remember to highlight the key points in your list of things to do, and don't bother with chitchat. They want to know the bottom line, not how you came up with your ideas. Give them specific goals to meet, but allow them to decide the process to accomplish that goal. Sometimes your only communication has to be the following:

- "We all have chores to do, so which ones would you prefer?"
- "You don't like us to remind you, so what systems can you put in place to remind yourself?"

Because they want to feel in charge, Prioritizers feel more comfortable when something has been measured, categorized, analyzed, or quantified in some way. They can quite easily find logical flaws in things people say and do at home and at work. Their mind tends to think inductively/deductively, and they tend to believe that everything has a logical explanation.

Give them limits, but let them make decisions whenever possible. They enjoy directing others and aren't fearful of others' challenges. Some even enjoy the debates! They can test almost everything to the limit. You may have some power struggles going on, as they want to be in control. They want results. Therefore, they like direct answers from you and straightforwardness.

They want to be in charge, so help them find ways to accomplish this.

They like work that uses their strong evaluation and decision-making skills and dislike tasks that are highly repetitious or that require strong interpersonal skills. They tend to assert themselves by directing others to meet their needs. They work fast but usually within control. Sometimes they may be defiant and think their way is the best way. They can become inflexible and often overcontrolling. Here are some tips that will help you deal with your bossy but hugely competent child:

• Be focused on the objectives and not the feelings.
• Focus on the joys of achievement.
• Be accountable for them.
• Don't ramble on. Speak logically.
• Include them in the decision-making process whenever possible.

Reward your Prioritizer for their ability to reason logically, for making decisions quickly and accurately, and for achieving their goals. They enjoy being acknowledged for their achievements, skill, and stamina. As you help them become more aware of the importance of getting organized, they will develop more confidence and eventually may self-motivate to set up and complete all kinds of chores around the house. Even though the Prioritizing child is hugely independent and comes off totally self-sufficient, they do need your support. Just be sure you always include them in your decision-making process. When you ask their opinion and put them in charge of important things to do, you will be amazed how these powerful personalities energetically run the show!

Heinrich Heine said his mother had lived in
dread of poetry, and snatched from him every
romance that she could out of his hands. And
she did everything possible to keep him from
superstition and poetry. Nevertheless, before
he was 16 he had written a number of verses.
—Catharine M. Cox, *Early Mental Traits*
of Three Hundred Geniuses

Prioritizers can come off a tad intense, dominant, and almost fierce at times. It is easy for other thinking styles to jump to conclusions and harshly judge the Prioritizer. Truth be told, "horse" children are not innately mean or insensitive; they just place their goals over other people's feelings. If the Maintainer, Harmonizer, or Innovator doesn't understand the Prioritizer's intention, they might feel snubbed or hurt. It would be great if Prioritizers could develop some patience and a tad of empathy so they could recognize everyone has their limitations and also grasp the truth; humanity isn't always sitting around waiting to serve them! But these goal-driven children are simply natural-born leaders, and they aren't concerned with being all warm and fuzzy. They want to get the job completed, and their competence and drive will pull it through, no matter how challenging or problematic.

Prioritizers rarely initiate conversations and tend to give recommendations first and ask questions later. They aren't really rude (although some would beg to differ), but because they are so impatient, they tend to spend more time giving orders than engaging others in their game plan. Prioritizers prefer to be the leaders, making all the decisions, calling all the shots, and bringing their project or team to victory.

The following list of adjectives describes the many facets of your Prioritizing-style child. They are not meant to pigeonhole him or her into a limited set of definitions, but rather, will paint a bigger picture to enable you to open your eyes to many of your child's particular gifts and talents. Notice how you view these traits. Some might seem negative at first read, so take a moment and consider the positive side as well. For example, *calculating* might seem inflexible and a big problem. Knowing more about who your child is and how they tick will inform and inspire new ways to communicate and relate with your Prioritizing child.

- Analytical
- Assertive
- Calculating
- Competitive
- Decisive
- Determined
- Direct

- Factual
- Goal-driven
- Logical
- Mathematical
- Objective
- Tenacious
- Thorough

When it comes to organizing, Prioritizers like to skip the details, get to the bottom line, and delegate the nitty-gritty to someone else. They can take cleaning up their room in small dosages only, especially if everyone knows they are committed to action. They'd like to walk out of their bedroom and get a big round of applause!

Prioritizers are easily bored with routine tasks, especially those that require multiple steps for completion. They want results *now*! Their best friend could be the Maintainer who, like the Prioritizer, thinks in a linear fashion but likes to support others, filling in the details without having to take the risks. Chances are, as children, they probably won't have anyone to delegate to, other than a friend, younger sibling, or a household pet, so look out! That doesn't mean they won't try!

As Prioritizers grow up, they often distinguish themselves by thriving at the fine art of living and are always striving for the best and to be the best. They are up-and-coming leaders who have the strength and determination to eventually see their goals come alive. They learn for a purpose and know what they want and how they are going to get it. Beware! Instead of getting out of their way, discover how you can support and encourage their drive and maybe even show them how to soften their growl once in a while. You catch more bees with honey than with turpentine!

How the Prioritizer Child Relates to Time

> The neurons that fire together wire together.
>
> —David Walsh, *WHY Do They Act That Way?*

The Prioritizer can be a master of time management. They will naturally set priorities and handle the most important tasks first and the least important last. They also have a natural ebb and flow of breaking tasks into smaller steps when necessary. Chances are, they have determined their weeknight and weekend bedtime and have even decided exactly when and where the family should go on a vacation. They are skilled at focusing whole-heartedly at the task at hand and managing their energy. They take time seriously and tend to show up a few minutes early for appointments and even school.

Prioritizers shine at . . . prioritizing, that's right! They have an innate sense of calculating and evaluating what needs to be done next to reach their goal. If you want them to get a gaggle of chores done, simply make the list—make bed, brush teeth, pick up toys, put away books—and then have them number which one they want to do first, second, third, and fourth. They are impatient, so watch out as they blast into action.

Prioritizers respect time and might preach, "There is no time to waste," or "Nothing like the present." If they are introverted, they will enjoy working alone and appreciate silence and their privacy. Home for the Prioritizing child isn't really seen as a place to entertain and have their friends over, but rather a place to think and set goals. They like taking things apart and seeing how everything works. Prioritizers want control over their surroundings. They also consistently make sure their things are in order, so don't you dare move their stuff!

The Prioritizing child tends to be somewhat frugal. They are careful how they spend their time as well as how they use their energy! Chances are, they will never leave a light on unnecessarily, and they will make sure they don't use too much water when showering. They are precise and committed to high quality, high ideals, and high principles. For them, time is worth its weight in gold, and they expect others to value time just as much as they do.

Prioritizers will stick to a project and make the most use of their time if it is important to them. For example, if having straight As, winning the soccer tournament, or gathering the most Halloween candy from house to house becomes a driving force in their life, it will run them and create purpose and passion.

Goals are important for everyone, but they are especially

important for the Prioritizing child. They give them clarity and focus and help them plan their day. Because they always want to make the most of their time, you can help them by asking them questions to clarify their purpose or interest. For example, write down some of their goals for the year on their calendar or encourage them to think about something positive they want to bring into their life, and have them draw a picture of it. Remember, Prioritizers appear to be mini-adults, but they are still kids! They may not always choose to put their intense energy in the best places! Help them understand what matters to them by working together to set their goals. Questions you might ask include the following:

- What are your current goals?
- Which one is the most important?
- What do you need to do first?
- How might your success help you and others?
- How will you know when you've achieved your goals?
- How can you organize your time to succeed?

Have your child write down their goals and then review them together. Help them focus on one or two. This process will not only assist them along their way, but also will allow you to keep connected and you'll be aware of what they are up to.

Your job is to help them discover time-saving solutions so they can accomplish the big things on their master list! If they aren't willing to listen to you, chance are, you are not providing them a discussion of the logical consequences of your suggestions. For example, if you say, "If you wait too long to get ready, you might miss outdoor playtime," or "If you don't pick up your clothes and take them to the laundry room right now, they will not be ready for your school concert tomorrow," they will more likely understand the reason to follow your lead. By seeing the purpose, they will do what it takes to save time.

Let's face it: they understand the value of time. If you interrupt them while they are working or playing, they won't like it—unless, of course, it is for a good logical reason. They want to be responsible, independent, and self-reliant, but at the same time they can be demanding and tenacious children. Be sure you set firm limits and make all your expectations clear. Otherwise, they'll want to do it their way.

Prioritizers don't know much about relaxing. They need to learn how to slow down and pace themselves. They may be driven to be the best, or want to shine at school, or just go, go, and go. Actually, they often underachieve at school, doing only what is necessary to achieve the goal, to pass, or to graduate. For their health and mental well-being, they need some downtime. Help them actually schedule one day a week in their calendar where nothing is planned. Or after school, be sure they unwind, play, and goof off for at least an hour or more. To make this work for them, during their free time, give them a list of things they are good at or things they would like to improve. That way they'll feel busy and engaged, but at least are taking a break from other, more competitive activities.

Lastly, remind them that you really appreciate how analytical and goal-oriented they take on tasks and responsibilities. Overtly applaud and reward their successes, but always be sure they can take a little time out to rest and recuperate.

"The Horse" at Home

> Children want to know that there are rules and
> timetables and right ways and wrong ways. I
> see it over and over again, when a child gets
> structure in his life, he [she] becomes happier,
> healthier, and more successful at everything
> he [she] does.
>
> —Dr. Edward Hallowell,
> *The Childhood Roots of Adult Happiness*

Prioritizers tend to have a lot of goals. They want to win and succeed at everything they do. It is important that their home supports their sense of control, order, and high standards for beauty and quality. Be sure you dedicate a place in their bedroom and the living room or den to display their awards and trophies. They desire few things, but what they choose needs to be the newest, the niftiest (they love gadgets), the highest quality, and the best buy for the money. They also like to know that all their school supplies, CD player, computer, and all appliances are in good working order. They also need extra supplies on hand. Don't worry; they won't usually waste resources, but be sure they have extra markers, pads, and Post-its. Prioritizers thrive in a highly functional environment. They prefer a neat and an uncluttered space, and love traditional black, white, navy, or gray colors—nothing flashy, please! Because they prefer to avoid clutter, their bedroom may look spartan or stark to their friends, but that is how they like it.

Because they like quality products and are attracted to the

best, if possible, let them buy their own stuff, including clothing and games. They are careful shoppers and will take time to inspect their potential purchase. They seldom make impulsive decisions and really will study up on the big-ticket item they want to buy. So unless you know exactly what they want, let them advise you. You are about to learn, or perhaps already know, that they don't mince words expressing what they like and what they don't like. If you are ever stumped, purchase them things that make them feel good about themselves, that boost their ego, or even frame their awards and buy nice display shelves to show them off! However, try not to take this all personally—they are just strong-minded kids!

Prioritizers are certainly not going to be the fashion trendsetters at school, because they have bigger things to tackle, like winning the debate contest or being the highest scorer on the basketball team. To keep their clothes organized, it is best to invest in a number of matching white plastic hangers. Help them organize their drawers by putting a different color or icon on the drawer handle and store what is appropriate inside. For example, if they are taking martial arts lessons, you can put a picture of the martial arts instructor on the drawer and they will know that that drawer keeps their sports/activity clothes together.

For their homework area, they need a functional workspace in which all their school supplies are easy to reach. Nothing can infuriate them more than having to look for missing pens or paper all over the house. It would be great if they had a separate area to study in or a special nook built into their bedroom. The kitchen table isn't ideal for them because they prefer not to share their school things with a sibling or even with you. They need to have all their supplies very handy. When it comes to getting their homework done, post a "Quiet, Study Zone" sign on their door so siblings won't interrupt. Also, they do well with a filing box for all their needs, classified by subject or month. Light blue, green, and natural colors enhance their studying experience by keeping the space feeling open and calm.

Prioritizers like to do things in their own way. If you understand their priorities, you won't have to lecture them to do this and that, but instead, can share a set of tasks to accomplish and get them engaged to logically pull them off. Like most children, they also appreciate rewards for a job well done. You certainly don't need to gift them with goodies, but solid words of encouragement, respect, and appreciation go a long way. They can be very self-motivated individuals. Certainly, they want your kind words, but they work hard to keep their space organized, not for emotional strokes, but rather so they can move forward on their path.

There may come a time when you have to inform them that it is not your job to organize the entire house; families must work together, and certain jobs must be delegated to get done. They may try to get out of having to wash dishes or do laundry, just like most children. Usually they have a hundred rational reasons why they should be exempt from the task at hand, readily delegating it to someone else. Nothing would make them happier than for you to do everything for them. You might have luck engaging them in the family chores by having them make the master list of things to do and then choosing three they are willing to tackle. That way they make the decisions and at least feel like the leader of their own set of tasks.

Prioritizers want home to be a private place where they can have peace and quiet and relax and unwind. A home for them isn't a place to be having a ton of sleepovers and friends over after school. They pretty much like to stick to themselves and have few social events, unless it is the principal of their school or their piano teacher. Listen to your Prioritizer. They'll tell you what they will and won't do. No beating around the bush here! Just realize it is your job to make them value what you say, as well. Once you come to verbal agreements, your Prioritizer child will get the job done with precision and diplomacy.

The Prioritizer Child at School

> Social not academic setback is what makes
> kids have a harder day.
>
> —Dr. Mel Levine, *Misunderstood Minds*

School is the place the Prioritizer shines. They love the recognition they receive from their classmates and teachers when they know the correct answers and do well on a test. They tolerate the traditional classroom because it is a means to an end. They tend to love the competition. They tend to work quickly and thoroughly and can do well in subjects that require the ability to reason, do critical analysis, and build strong logical arguments. Many teachers can see the little academic researcher or professor emerging.

Because they handle numbers easily, chances are they handle math well and may end up with a CPA or MBA. They also gravitate toward figuring out how all things work and may enjoy public speaking. They like to play the devil's advocate, as it practices their analytical skills. They may become the best debaters their school ever produced or win all the science competitions!

They like to be admired for their brilliance and their contribution to the intellectual realm much more than who they are or who they hang out with.

Prioritizers are often articulate, even when quite young, and may even intimidate a teacher or two. They give the teacher a good run for the money, as they are not afraid of confrontation, especially if they are sure they are right! Opinionated and strongly committed to their goals, the Prioritizer will persist in the face of most difficulties. Many see school as game, one that must be won to be successful. They can be workaholics who prefer to work alone, but if they have to lead and motivate their fellow students, they do it convincingly and with a lot of gusto. They like speaking up and doing class presentations, which make them appear to others to be a natural-born leader who prefers to administrate projects rather than manage the details. They don't like "doing things by committee" and some students may feel Prioritizers are too assertive and directive.

In school, they need to learn some social skills to develop sensitivity to other people's feelings. They aren't even aware of them often! Sometimes they are too impatient with others' slower performance, and too critical. They may come across as unemotional and uncaring. Yes, they are power-driven and autocratic. What's a parent to do? Try to create an opportunity when they come home from school to debrief, especially to discuss social interactions. Over time, you can help them realize that others simply aren't as goal-oriented or self-assured as they are.

Prioritizers like to be viewed as number one. Therefore, they need to find subjects and activities in which they can direct and take charge. With school, they are much more concerned with getting the answer right than being the most popular student.

They are not afraid to express their ideas and have strong ideas about each and every topic. Prioritizers tend to be opinionated and can be harsh and unfeeling to other people, including their school chums. Because they work, move, and think quickly, they don't have time for chitchat, and many undervalue the importance of personal relationships. This may be to the dismay of their classmates and to the teachers, as they aren't afraid to challenge anyone. Watch out! The general is marching down the hallway!

The Prioritizer at Play

> Rene Descartes—French philosopher—was determined, even before his 16th year to search only for truth, and in mathematics, begun at about this time, he believed he had found the goal he was seeking. Before he was 8 years old his father called him the "little philosopher."
>
> —Catharine M. Cox, *Early Mental Traits of Three Hundred Geniuses*

Prioritizers need physical exercise because it is one of the few ways they actually release their stress and relax. They enjoy large muscle activities like running races, playing tag, and hide-and-seek because they require skill, stamina, and the desire to win, win, win. Just like the lion, they enjoy the chase! Basic work is play for them. They like the element of work being a component in their play and like to be busy, fixing things and making a difference.

Prioritizers also enjoy intellectual games. For example, you can help them develop a financial plan and teach them about spending and saving based on their weekly allowance. They also like the fun of being navigator for the next family car trip or preparing a survival kit for family camping trips. They may be honored to lead the family weekly meetings but not writing up the agenda—a job that would be better situated for the Maintaining-style child. They also have the ability to focus on a craft project or play with a toy for a very long time. They like to take things apart and then put them back together. They need to understand the relationship between things and how something works as a whole. They are intrigued by that and need fewer things to play with overall.

Telling them that something is going to be fun isn't enough to get them going. They need to know why something they are about to commit to will advance their grades at school or make them more successful in another way. The Prioritizer loves verbal sparing, and engaging in lively debates tickles their fancy. Trouble is, play for them is ultimately about winning and building confidence. They can become insensitive and a tad mean when they lose at something.

It is obvious that this kind of child isn't a typical playmate! Because everything is intensely competitive, they need to find kids who appreciate a good leader and are willing to be led. Chances are, they will have a few select friends who must be capable, useful, goal-oriented, and who are not emotionally needy. It makes sense that Prioritizers aren't that big on social functions, unless they can meet someone valuable and gain something by it. Thus, they are oblivious to the "messages" conveyed in their nonverbal gestures or tone of voice. They aren't going to pay attention to your feelings much, either. The name of the game is, "Don't take it personally." If you do, you'll suffer. When you don't, you can really enjoy this mighty powerful child.

Nurturing Your Prioritizing-Style Child

> I have the simplest of taste; I am always satisfied with the best.
>
> —Oscar Wilde, *www.brainyquote.com*

The Prioritizing child is always on the go. Whether they are at home, school, or beyond, they are always driven to win and achieve goals. They are self-motivated and eager to move quickly toward their numerous goals and dreams. Prioritizers are intelligent, determined, and want to excel. They are driven mini-adults—a tall order for any parent or caregiver to guide and handle.

When it comes to the realm of organizing, Prioritizers prefer to delegate rather than get caught up in the humdrum of little tasks. If they had their druthers, they would do minimal house chores and simply keep their own stuff working and clean. Because their self-esteem rises when they are able to set and achieve goals, Prioritizers do well when you give them specific, reasonable challenges. Remember, they don't take things personally, so they can be gently cajoled into doing those things they don't want to do. If they understand how important it is to you, they will leap into action and accomplish the task with zest and determination. However, I highly doubt it!

Don't forget, the more say they have in determining how they approach tasks one, two, and three, the more willing they are to do it. Give your Prioritizing child simple, strategic doses of organizing advice. Do not overwhelm them with the details, but stick to solid structures for setting up systems. The Prioritizing child needs freedom within restrictions and guidance without restraint.

Prioritizing Style: Lion Overview

Purpose: To set and achieve goals.

Organization of space: They like things to function well and want their things to be in a logical space. They prefer to delegate the organizing jobs.

Strengths: Good at making the best use of their time. Tend to be hyperfocused and driven at accomplishing a meaningful goal.

Challenges: They prefer not to do any organizing if possible. They will only do it if they see the value in it. They are also not that sensitive to people's feelings.

Prioritizing Style: Time

Calendar: Has the ability to keep pretty much in their own head, but strongly rely on others for help.

To-do list: Has the ability to keep pretty much of their to-dos in their head, but may have a master goal list going on.

Goals: To get the most use of their time and to get the most done.

Strengths: Very good at time management, punctual—maybe a couple minutes early, functions at a high level.

Challenges: Wants to make decisions and be in charge. Has difficulty accommodating to anyone else's schedule.

Prioritizing Style: Home

Bedroom: Prefers to have minimal things, but in order. Accolades may be welcomed on walls, and awards are predominately placed.

Closets: Prefers to have a clean, aesthetic with matching hangers and everything in perfect order.

Drawers: What little they own, they like to have easily accessible and have few but the best.

Memorabilia: Tends to keep things that denote victory and success, like athletic or academic awards.

Storage: Would like to spend their allowance money on tools and equipment. They want functional storage with a minimal of upkeep.

Strengths: A pristine, functional environment.

Challenges: Want to delegate maintaining.

Prioritizing Style: School

Homework: Does whatever is necessary to meet goals, and works diligently in a quiet area with minimal distraction.

Strengths: Is a goal-oriented student.

Challenges: Managing emotions and feelings and being told what to do.

Easy Ways to Get Your Prioritizer Child Organized

- Give them options, and let them decide what should be done. However, stick around to see if they need help.

- Be logical, not emotional, when telling them to get organized.
- Don't buy them things unless you know what they want. It is best to give them birthday money and then they'll make up their mind.
- Buy them the best but few.
- Because they like facts and figures, give them strict directions and the time it should take to get organized. The more specific, the better.
- They appreciate keeping their toys and supplies in good working order. Respect that quality, and help them when things aren't working.
- They prefer to keep things together by subject or type, not by alphabetic or numerical order.
- Be creative with storage. They are more concerned with quick access than simply aesthetics.
- Be willing to have them delegate things to you. Encourage them by helping them create a delegation list.
- Encourage them to take time off to enjoy life and not just work in attaining their never-ending goals!

CHAPTER 6

The Role of Sensory Preference

> Rats develop bigger, thicker, and more com-
> plex nerve systems when kept in cages
> equipped with a variety of rat toys—running
> wheels and mazes. The dissected brains of
> other rats, which have been kept either in
> more spartan cages or in conditions of sensory
> deprivation do not show the same complex
> development of connections in the threads
> of the brain.
>
> —Anne Moir and David Jessel,
> *Brain Sex*

In addition to a thinking style, each of us has a sensory preference. Unfortunately, parents and teachers are often unaware of
the unique way we take in the world and express ourselves, and
sometimes they impose their own sensory preferences on us.
When they do, things can get difficult or tense. A client of mine
confessed, "I wish my parents would have had this book when
I was little! I was a real kinesthetic child, seemingly so wild and
unruly compared to them. My mom was extremely visual, and
everything was about appearances. My dad was auditory, and he
was so sensitive to every little sound I'd make. And there I was
dancing and turning the carpets upside down to explore and enjoy my life! We drove each other crazy, just because we were all
so different."

Sensory differences can create chaos in a household if not understood. Carol Kranowitz states in her book, *The Out-of-Sync Child,* "children often express extremes of too much sensitivity or not enough sensitivity in one of the three sensory preferences." Either way, enormous challenges can develop in our children's lives. They may not be seen or known for who they are; they might be overly expressed in that area and need to balance out; and of course, they aren't always given what they really require to help them thrive. The goal, I believe, is to achieve what is called full functional sensory integration. According to the authors of *The Sensory-Sensitive Child,* "Sensory integration is the delicate interaction between the brain and body . . . it is nothing short of marvelous. It allows us to move purposefully through the world without being driven to distraction . . . your body is working for you, not against you . . . we live what we sense." Do many of us really take into consideration what sense really works best for us? Do many of us know where to find our inherent sensory home, the place that helps us find comfort, strength, and make sense of things in our surroundings? Ask yourself:

- *Do you remember things best seen outside or read in a book? Or do you feel you just need to write down everything?*
- *Do you need to talk through problems to solve them?*
- *Do you like to learn through diagrams, pictures, and even demonstrations?*
- *Do you learn new words by actually spelling them out loud, seeing them, or hearing them?*

Let's use learning the alphabet as an example. If you are auditory, you might sing your way through the ABCs. If you are visual, you enjoy looking at the letters. If you are kinesthetic, you might relish writing the letters over and over or even dancing them! Which expression do you or your child display?

Our brain takes in sensory stimuli from sensory receptors that enter our central nervous system and decodes so that we can better understand our experiences. The brain can decode more than ten million bits of sensory data per second. Our brains contain more than 100 billion nerve cells. Some of these cells, called neurons, decode the information, bringing us experiences of sensation in all its forms. Ultimately, our senses pervade every aspect of our lives and give us a home base, like safe bedrock, to discover new things and encourage growth and positive changes. Naturally, knowing which sense is our preference can help us establish a kind of personal compass that gives direction for how we relate to other people, our homes, and our creativity.

Our senses not only give us pleasure, but they also help us learn about our inner and outer world. As the brain analyzes and interprets what is happening outside of us as we see colors, hear the wind, even touch a peach, we take it all in and develop a relationship with our personal experiences that leads us into a better understanding of our inner world. It starts really early. A baby in its first four months of life typically links up with all its sensory and motor functions, and by the eighth month can actually interpret by motioning their hands or moving to an object by what they see, hear, and touch.

How Sensory Preference Affects Organizing Style

Whatever sense our children naturally prefer to operate from—be it visual, auditory, or kinesthetic—that sense influences which organizing system at home and at school will work the best. I assure you, knowing your child's sensory preference will enhance organizing success. If children feel comfortable in a certain environment and internally validated, they will want to stay in that room and do the necessary work, or play games and socialize.

With all the sensations coming into our nervous system on a moment-to-moment basis, we tend to feel comfortable and desire to be in environments that support our sensory preference. Children often feel better in some rooms or homes or public spaces than in others because their senses are being rewarded, they are being validated, and they feel safe and sound. When we know our children's preference, we can provide a home and family milieu that brings ease and safety and promotes relaxation and creativity.

How does knowing someone's sensory preference help him or her organize better? According to Mihaly Csikszentmihalyi, author of *Flow,* when the mind is fully present in an activity, the person's mental and physical performance levels soar. Going with what comes naturally is the smartest way to live, love, and organize. And it means less stress in getting the job done. Because you as parent are in charge, you are able to set the tone and create an environment that really resonates with your child. It will turn out to be a space they want to inhabit and will dissipate tendencies of procrastination to help them energize and support work and play with joy and ease. Let's face it: knowing what stimulates and supports your child, and what makes them perform better with less energy, is what identifying sensory preferences is all about.

What Is My Child's Sensory Preference?

Instructions

Read each of the following statements and check the responses that most resonate with what your child would do in any given situation. Add up the total number of check marks at the bottom of each section. An explanation can be found below. Arlene Taylor, Ph.D., of Realizations, Inc., created the test. (Used by permission.) For further information, please view the Sensory Preference Assessment in my previous book, *Organizing for Your Brain Type.*

Section One

My child . . .

_____ Likes pets that make sounds or talk and prefers toys that make sounds.

_____ Requires that foods "sound right" (e.g., may like or dislike the way food sounds when being chewed).

_____ Is often afraid of loud or unfamiliar sounds (e.g., storms, sirens, people crying).

_____ Focuses on the way clothing sounds (e.g., may like/dislike swish of nylon or clank of zippers).

_____ Is often sensitive to things he or she hears in the environment (e.g., caregivers arguing, a child being punished).

_____ Tends to quickly feel nurtured/loved by positive auditory stimuli (e.g., pleasant sounds in nature, pleasing music, affirming voice tones).

_____ May feel hurt by lack of positive auditory input (e.g., silent treatment, harsh voices, jangling keys, raucous/unpleasant noises).

_____ Often learns most quickly by hearing verbal explanations of how something is done.

_____ Enjoys writing things down and taking notes.

Prefers to fall asleep to music or white noise.

Section One Total = _____

Section Two

My child . . .

_____ Likes pets that are interesting to watch and may prefer colorful, attractive toys that move.

_____ Requires that food must "look right" (e.g., may dislike beets and mashed potatoes blending into each other on plate).

_____ Is often afraid of the dark or of shadows.

_____ Is often afraid when watching videos, movies, and pictures they perceive as scary.

_____ Feels appearance is very important (e.g., may be bothered by tattered, worn, mended, or outmoded clothes).

_____ Is often sensitive to things he or she sees in the environment (e.g., facial expressions, shadowing on the wall).

_____ Tends to feel nurtured/loved by positive visual stimuli (e.g., visually pleasing environments, affirming eye contact or facial expressions).

_____ May feel hurt by lack of eye contact, angry facial expressions, visually unpleasant surroundings, lack of things to look at.

_____ Often learns most quickly by seeing (watching) how something is done.

_____ Prefers diagrams, charts, and pictures when learning.

Section Two Total = _____

Section Three

My child . . .

_____ Likes pets that are comfortable to touch and may be very sensitive/intuitive with animals.

_____ Prefers toys that feel good (e.g., smooth, soft, interesting texture).

_____ Requires that foods must "feel right" (e.g., not too hot or cold, not scratchy, not slimy).

_____ Is often afraid of any type of pain, physical irritation, or discomfort.

_____ Focuses on the way clothing feels (e.g., soft against the skin, restrictive, sweaty).

_____ Is often sensitive to the way things feel in the environment (e.g., temperature, drafts of wind, furniture).

_____ Tends to quickly feel nurtured/loved by gentle, affirming touch and environments that feel comfortable.

_____ May feel hurt by lack of touch or harsh touch (e.g., spanked, slapped, kicked, jerked, hair pulled, held down and tickled).

_____ Often learns most quickly by actually touching and doing.

_____ Tends to problem-solve by engaging their hands, for example, when telling a story or solving a math problem.

Section Three Total = _____

Put totals from each section in the corresponding boxes. The highest score typically represents sensory preference.

Section 1—Auditory	Section 2—Visual	Section 3—Kinesthetic

Your Auditory Child

> The first of the child's organs to begin
> functioning are his senses.
>
> —Maria Montessori, *The Absorbent Mind*

Auditory children relate to sound more sensitively than to other stimuli. They are keenly aware of what they hear in their surroundings and react not only to the content of words, but also can be stimulated, relaxed, or annoyed by pitch, volume, and intonations. Some auditory children concentrate best when it is silent; others seem to need a steady flow of background sound to help them think. Many auditories do well with a sound machine generating white noise, which helps mask the distracting sounds of a busy classroom or uncomfortable noises in their homes. (Tip: Putting carpet in their rooms and even soundproofing can help them relax and sleep better.) Many early tweens love having music on when doing their homework and especially when getting organized! Music helps these kids remain calm, focused, and on task.

You know you are with an auditory child when they say, "I *hear* what you are saying," or "Gee, that *sounds* great!" They tend to learn more easily when they hear an explanation rather than seeing it demonstrated or even doing it themselves. They also prefer working and playing where people are talking a lot. Auditories also appreciate positive auditory stimulation such as the sound of birds or words spoken in gentle tones. Because they have intense listening skills, auditory children enjoy verbal discussions. When you want to get them organized, engage them in a conversation about how cleaning up their room might improve how they feel. When they start listening and resonating with the sound of your voice, they'll be up for anything.

How you name and categorize things is very important to the success and longevity of how you organize your auditory child. (They can hear words in their head before they can speak or write them down.) Because your child appreciates words, spend an adequate amount of time labeling their stuff. It will make all the difference in the world. Rhyming words and using word games will also help them remember where you put things, and verbalizing their location out loud will reinforce their memory and interest.

For example, when organizing their homework binder, put things in alphabetical or subject related together. Or when getting their things ready for summer camp, have a list they can make up that is subject related, from activities to clothing, but that they can check off. You may even want to tape-record them reading out loud a list of those things you put away in certain containers for long-term storage so they can listen at a future date to hear and remember what's what and where.

The key skill to cultivate when parenting and organizing an auditory child is how to give specific, concise directions, spoken clearly and with a gentle tone. You may need to repeat the instructions, but your child will eventually remember. Because they enjoy vocal sounds, like whistling or even singing, try to make your words rhythmic and play with the intonations. I encourage all the senses to have a sleep and play space that reflects their unique needs. Because sounds grab the auditories' attention more than the colors of a painting or the feel of a cashmere sweater, try to have a fountain running or a stereo playing in the background of any room you want them to inhabit. For some auditory children, just put on a Hillary Duff CD, and they will be stacking boxes and putting away toys in a jiffy.

Setting the Mood for the Auditory Child
- Give them verbal instructions to an organizing problem.
- Encourage them to talk through their organizing issues.
- They tend to be great listeners; therefore, be mindful at what you ask of them.
- They may enjoy listening to music while organizing.
- They may learn new words or ideas by listening to the rhythm of the words rather than looking at written material.
- They tend to remember things by writing them down or drawing a map where their things are.

Your Visual Child

Visual children take in the world around them through sight. They like color and bright and aesthetically pleasing things, and they draw conclusions about something by how it looks rather than how it sounds or feels. Visual children are sensitive to your facial expressions. Be aware of this when scolding or appreciating, and express what you want to express with forethought. They also

Play a lifelong game of people pleasing, all the
while suppressing their true selves, to the
point that as adults they have no feeling of
who they really are.

—Dr. Edward Hallowell,
The Childhood Roots of Adult Happiness

learn by watching how something is done rather than by actively
participating in it. Visuals often talk rapidly and use a multitude
of visual metaphors such as "Let's take a *look* at this!" or "I can
see it perfectly clear."

Children with a visual preference love color. It inspires
them, and if their bedroom walls are painted in colors they enjoy,
it will really help them feel comfortable yet productive. Brightly
colored toys and lavish colors in their picture books can make
them feel calmer, while also engaging their attention. How something looks is more important than how it is placed and in what
area of the room it is in. Color can unify their approach and make
them feel jazzed up and motivated. The look over the function
will be what they focus on.

Visual children require a specific organizing system to ensure their success and happiness. They can be overly sensitive or
excited if too many things are hanging or cluttering their space.
Take time to plan out the colors of their room as well as exactly
what will go where. Be sure there is a large colorful garbage can
so any clutter can be done away with immediately, before it
makes them edgy. Determine what colors suit them in all areas,
and help them make choices. For example, you might want to
help them choose just the right color folder for their classes; say
blue for science and green for math. This will be a big help in

motivating them to take out the color they identify to do their homework! It's that simple. I would also like to encourage you to give your visual child a room with windows. A view into the garden can bring your child great peace and delight.

Space planning a room for visual children is very important. Moving furniture inspires change, and visuals love to get involved in making things in their room look different. It not only freshens things up, but it also forces them to deal with all their stuff hidden under their bed! (I'm not a big fan of storing things under the bed anyway, unless there is a total lack of space.) The look must be pleasing or your visual won't want to spend any time in their bedroom. Also, because the visual enjoys communicating with people in person rather than over the phone, be sure their bedrooms accommodate guests. Two more tips: be sure their study area is clear of clutter, and put full-spectrum light-bulbs into all lamps. Visuals thrive when the lighting is healthy and bright.

When you decide to organize your visual child, schedule short, frequent organizing sessions instead of committing to one long gruesome day. They get easily discouraged when things are in chaos, so try not to tell them to organize their whole bedroom at once. Start in stages—remove the toys off the floor, then hang up their clothes, then clear their desks. Start small and supervise, but let them be in charge of where things go.

Visuals do well with containerizing. They love uniform plastic baskets that will assist them in noticing and using what they have and will make them want to use their organizing system because it looks so darn good! Put colored baskets in their closet as well. Not that I advocate going shopping, but purchasing nice, attractive containers goes without saying for the visual. If they like the look of it, they are bound to use it. Noting the color and quality of the new organizing gadgets can be a deal-breaker for the visual children out there!

Setting the Mood for the Visual Child

- They tend to be sensitive to how things are placed in their environment.
- They tend to be sensitive to lighting and may appreciate dim lighting when doing their homework.
- They tend to learn by demonstration. Show them how to fold their clothes or retrieve documents in their files. They become impatient or even bored when extensive listening is required of them.
- They tend to be receptive to attractive or colorful organizing containers and supplies.
- They tend to like things perfectly labeled.
- Hang motivation posters to encourage them to get organized.
- Use big corkboards or chalkboards for upcoming events or regular planned activities.
- Use a big magnet board to store memorabilia on their walls in their playroom or their bedroom.
- Things are much better in the open but must be well placed or hidden with a curtain or behind the door.

Your Kinesthetic Child

Comfort is the key word for the kinesthetic child. They learn about the world by touching every square inch and often express themselves by saying, "That doesn't **feel** right" or "My gut is telling me something . . ." The brain's outer territory is the skin,

> By the time the child is 5 years old, the brain
> will have reached almost 90 percent of its final
> size, but it will keep developing well into his
> adolescence.
>
> —Karen A. Smith and Karen R. Gouze,
> *The Sensory-Sensitive Child*

covered with 70 percent of our sensory receptors. We know that babies who are not given tactile stimulation have more complications growing up. It is obvious how important it is to acknowledge and validate the kinesthetic child for their sensory preference.

Because they are sensitive to the touch, kinesthetics are easily irritated, and physical discomfort can make them pull away from situations or individuals. These children do well surrounded by stuffed animals, with a baby blanket or two around, or being cuddled and held. They crave physical stimulation. It's a good idea to be sure kinesthetic children's bedrooms are furnished with comfortable, soft, friendly furniture. Their bedrooms need to make them feel good, and if they feel comfortable and nurtured at their desks and in their beds, they will relax and exhibit signs of peace and calm. Kinesthetic children are also sensitive to taste and smell, so be sure their rooms are fresh and aired out, and be careful about choosing before-bed snacks.

Because kinesthetics learn best through movement and touch, they are sometimes misdiagnosed as hyperactive or ADHD (attention deficit/hyperactivity disorder). Truth be told, if these kids can't hold it, feel it, or pick it up, it doesn't exist. Instead of judging them unruly, recognize this active behavior is simply an expression of their sensory preference. Nothing is wrong! On that note, be sure their rooms have carpeting that will provide warmth, support, and something tactile to engage. They may also enjoy textured fabric for their bedspread and a nice thick blotter on their desk. Anything that gives them more sensory experience adds depth to their experience and greater learning.

Kinesthetics are rather "antsy" types, and it follows that they enjoy doing the physical, work-related organizing. They are so talented when it comes to bodily coordination, so doing things that requires them to use their hands will be embraced and done well. They actually thrive on touching things, so get them to box up stuff, have them zip into the garage and put things away, and invite them back to do more work!

Kinesthetics also like to keep their environment "controlled." They want the temperature controlled, the windows open, and clutter kept to not just the bare minimum. Comfort is a key concern. Therefore, a commitment to getting and staying organized would help that kinesthetic out a lot. Having certain things in certain rooms and making sure it all *feels* right are totally important.

Setting the Mood for the Kinesthetic Child

- They tend to learn how to get organized by touching and feeling their things and appropriately placing them.
- They tend to attack problem-solving physically, impulsively, and in motion.
- They tend to be sensitive to the physical touch, and organizing containers will be used if they are comfortable to touch.
- They tend to be sensitive to temperature.

- They tend to gather and place things in no particular order, encouraging room for other things to be added too.
- They tend to do well when things are placed easier for them to touch and to use.

Sensory Preference: Summary

> Most people use all their senses to learn
> things, and they don't learn in only one way.
> But some students find that they learn better
> in one way than in others. It can be advanta-
> geous, which learning style works best for you.
> —Elizabeth James and Carol Barkin,
> *How to Be School Smart*

No matter your child's sensory preference, the more in tune with what sense works the best, the better. Structure breeds safety, and the security this brings leads to them blossoming and thriving in new ways. Kids fidget less when they feel grounded and are less nervous; they find more control and balance in themselves and their environment. When kids are less distracted, their social skills and their studies improve as well. Using their sensory preference as a frame of reference in establishing an organizing routine or when space planning their bedroom also helps you make their life easier and more enjoyable. Knowing what helps them stay organized will also give you more time in your life to do things you really want to do.

As Maria Montessori pointed out, "Nothing comes to the intellect that is not first in the senses." A child's environment should invite him or her in, providing a welcoming space and setting in which to learn, grow, and feel at home. Parents who understand and honor their child's preferred sensory preference have the insights to create just that type of environment.

CHAPTER 7

The Role of Extroversion and Introversion

> A hypersensitive or painfully shy child will remember interactions with his parents differently than an outgoing, extroverted kid for whom childhood was a fearless, playful romp.
> —Dan Kindlon, Ph.D., *Too Much of a Good Thing*

Our relative comfort level in any given environment is partly related to how much stimulation our brains can handle easily. Or to put it in another way, our position is based on a metaphorical extroversion-introversion continuum. Extroverted children, for example, draw their energy from others and things and need lots of feedback and verbal affirmation when doing something new. Chances are, they may even want a parent to be close by so they can share experiences and ideas. Isolation for them is tough, never mind doing something they don't want to do, like organizing! Obviously, the trick is to organize *with* your extroverted kids. It will make all the difference.

By contrast, introverted children draw energy from being inside themselves and from being with one or two special people. New situations, settings, or unfamiliar people can challenge them. Too many people can zap their energy, and they need oodles of space and tremendous amounts of time alone. The trick for organizing your introverted child is to gently guide him or her into the process to avoid draining their energy. But more on that later.

Interestingly enough, studies of the brain show that introverts have long, complex blood flow paths in their brain, which indicate more internal stimulation. The introvert focuses internally and may engage in long or complex inner scenarios, thoughts, or reflections when solving problems. Extroverts' blood flow has shorter, more direct pathways in the brain. Extroverts respond more to what occurs externally. As a result, they prefer high levels of stimulation that make them feel comfortable and nurtured.

You might be pausing to think, "Aha. My child is an extrovert. That's why she is always on the phone or wanting to invite the entire class over for her birthday party." Or "I get it. My child is an introvert. That's why he disappears in his room when people come over to visit." Remember, this isn't about having proper social skills; instead, it is about understanding your child's basic needs and then creating a support system that works for them. You'll learn to orchestrate social activities appropriately for each type of child. Because you can't change your child's preference (to be more like you, perhaps), how can you give equal time to both the out-loud, dramatic extrovert and the quieter introverts at the dinner table? Get a "talking stick" and let everyone at the table pass it around to take an official turn at telling about his or her day. Any stick will do . . . I suggest a branch, a gong, or a family memento. It's a great way to celebrate your differences!

For our purposes, I have chosen to portray extroversion-introversion as a 70-30 continuum. I've taken the extreme extroverts and two-third of the ambiverts and called them "extroverts," and I've taken the extreme introverts and the high end of ambiversion and called them "introverts." This may not be an accurate representation of brain function, but it does reflect society's emphasis and reward to extroverts who get out there and "do," versus the introverts who "be and think." This is a very complex topic. The majority of children have somewhat balanced needs to stimulation versus relief from stimulation. But there are children at the extreme ends of the continuum who need a great deal of stimulation versus those who need a great deal of protection from too much stimulation. Parents and teachers can often pick out the extremes rather easily, and if the child doesn't fall into the extreme category, there is a likelihood that child is an ambivert.

QUIZ

Child Extroversion-Introversion Assessment

Instructions:
Consider each row of statements, and choose the one (A, B, or C) that *applies to your child at least 75 percent of the time.* When you're finished, tally the totals for each response. The column with the highest score will give you some idea of whether your child is extremely extroverted, ambiverted, or extremely introverted.

©2003 by Arlene Taylor, Ph.D.   www.arlenetaylor.org
Realizations, Inc.

A	B	C
A Is extremely competitive with others	B Is moderately competitive with self or others	C Is rarely competitive with others (may compete with self)
A Tends to be energized by competition	B Tends to handle moderate amounts of competition well	C Tends to become energy-depleted by competition (avoids it when possible)
A Tends to be energized by large groups of people	B Tends to prefer moderate-sized groups of people for moderate periods of time	C Tends to become exhausted by large groups of people
A Tends to recover very quickly when exhausted	B Tends to recover moderately quickly when exhausted	C Tends to recover very slowly when exhausted
A Tends to go, go, go and often has to be encouraged to relax	B Prefers activities and relaxation time in about a 50-50 ratio	C Tends to prefer activities done alone or with few people
A Tends to gravitate toward highly stimulating environments (e. g., lots of action, noise, people, color, sound, sports)	B Tends to gravitate toward moderately stimulating environments	C Tends to gravitate toward quiet environments where there is little outside stimulation (e.g., nature)
A Tends to jump in and "take a risk" to participate in a new environment or situation	B Tends to participate some of the time and to just observe some of the time	C Tends to hang back and "observe" rather than participate, especially in a new environment or situation
A Tends to crave high levels of stimulation	B Tends to crave moderate amounts of stimulation alternated with relief from stimulation	C Tends to distance from high levels of stimulation
A Prefers to do activities with a large group	B Prefers to do activities with a small group of individuals	C Prefers to do activities alone or with just one or two others

A	B	C
Tends to respond to environments with low levels of sensory stimulation by becoming very active	Tends to respond best to environments with moderate levels of sensory stimulation	Tends to respond to environments with high levels of sensory stimulation by withdrawing
Tends to become bored and may fall asleep in nonstimulating environments	Tends to respond best to moderate amounts of stimulation in the environment	Tends to withdraw and may become sick in overstimulating environments
Tends to get into trouble easily (e.g., trying to find something stimulating to do)	Tends to like activities but isn't on a "mission" to continually find something exciting to do	Tends to get depressed easily (e.g., with continued pressure to participate)
Tends to perform better in busy/noisy environments	Tends to handle busy/noisy environments for a while but then needs to balance with a quiet environment	Tends to perform better in quiet environments
Tends to be very interactive with the environment	Tends to be interactive balanced with contemplative periods	Tends to be very contemplative
Tends to want music playing in the environment most of the time	May want music playing some of the time and may want quiet half of the time	Tends to want the environment quiet, especially when studying or trying to concentrate
Tends to have good short-term memory but may forget things in the long term	Moderately good short-term and long-term memory	Tends to have good long-term memory but may have difficulty recalling things under stress (exams)
Tends to be quite bold when confronted with new people or situations	Tends to be moderate in response when confronted with new people or situations	Tends to be very cautious when confronted with new people or situations
Tends to be very quick to adapt	Tends to be moderate in capacity to adapt	Tends to be slow to adapt

A	B	C
Tends to have a positive response to new stimuli	Tends to have a mild positive or negative response to new stimuli	Tends to have a negative response to new stimuli
Tends to explore new situations without hesitation	Tends to be intermediate in terms of exploring or clinging	Tends to cling to the familiar (e.g., mother) for much longer in new situations
Tends to be relatively insensitive to input through the five senses and can take tremendous amounts of stimulation before has had enough	Tends to be moderately sensitive to input through the five senses	Tends to be highly sensitive to input through the five senses and requires very little stimulation before has had enough
Tends to be more difficult to "train" and may be very rebellious	Tends to be moderately easy to "train" and may be moderately rebellious	Tends to be easier to "train" and may not evidence much overt rebellion
Total number of A responses ____ Extroverted	Total number of B responses ____ Ambiverted	Total number of C responses ____ Introverted

Your Extroverted Child

> We want to understand children not renovate
> them.
>
> —Alison Gopnik, Andrew Meltzoff and Patricia Kuhl,
>
> *The Scientist in the Crib*

- *Why does she have forty best friends?*
- *Can't he ever stop talking?*
- *Why does she speak so quickly all of the time?*
- *Why does he always need to be the center of attention?*
- *Why does she have to brainstorm out loud?*
- *Why does he talk first and then think later?*

Let's look at extroverted Claire. She's an eleven-year-old who is either constantly on the phone or entertaining a ton of friends. When she has to organize her CDs or start her homework after school, she procrastinates and usually gets nothing done. She seeks out distractions—listening to music or having the radio on, watching TV, or instant messaging. She can multitask like no other if there is something to bounce to on her boom box, and she may need that external stimulation to motivate her to do something she doesn't want to do.

Extroverts draw their energy from other people, things, and various outside influences. They prefer to engage in the world around them by sharing ideas and personal experiences. Extroverts appreciate other people and their ideas so much that it nurtures, energizes, and uplifts their spirits. If they don't have the opportunity to talk and be around people, they may feel like they are running out of energy and can become cranky and demanding. Seemingly flighty or ungrounded extroverted children can have a hard time and are often misunderstood. There are just too many thoughts going on in their heads, all the time. Often extroverted children have a difficult time doing their homework (they are thinking about too many things) or falling asleep at night (they are thinking about too many things). Parents can help their extrovert children by being around them while they do their homework to create a more social atmosphere and by putting them to bed at night with a bed or room full of stuffed animals and books. This kind of lavish attention will make them feel comforted, relaxed, and at peace. Remember that their need for material possession and having your approval doesn't come from low self-esteem. Rather, it is an essential way they thrive.

Organizing Your Extroverted Child

• When it comes to organizing, extrovorted children need to receive lots of verbal input, compliments, and encouragement
while in the process. Verbal affirmations work well for them,
and even when you think your cheerleading voice has had it,
give them more!

• When they come home from school, they are the ones who
jump off the school bus, run into the house, and chatter on and
on about their day. Be ready for them. Open the door and welcome them home. Invite them to talk and share their experiences.

• If you can be around and guide your extroverts in keeping
their backpacks from getting unruly or making sure their
clothes are hung up and toys are off the floor, they will have an
easier time doing it. They enjoy and need to interact with you.
Support them, but don't get in their way. And keep the cheerleading going!

• They enjoy being around people or their things. Working with
them or being in the background will encourage them to plow
ahead in organizing their stuff.

• They tend to let you know and share when things aren't going
well when they are organizing. They will always let you know
what they are thinking and feeling. Give them an opportunity
to express themselves when they are going about their organizing.

• They need a lot of approval and coaching when it comes to getting organized.

• When they don't get their things organized, don't punish them
by sending them to their room alone. That is difficult for them.

Your Introverted Child

> The scientific studies into what makes for
> happiness both in childhood and in adulthood
> always emphasize that it is crucial to feel that
> you have control over yourself and your
> environment.
>
> —Dr. Edward Hallowell,
> *The Childhood Roots of Adult Happiness*

- *Why does he take so long to respond to a question?*
- *Why does she hate being interrupted?*
- *Why doesn't he like large group activities?*
- *Why is she so shy and reserved?*
- *Why do people drain him?*

Sam is an eight-year-old introvert. He thrives on one-to-one conversations but has a hard time staying connected when another kid comes into the conversation. People think Sam is bored or disinterested. Actually, he is thinking silently in his head, not like Claire, who thinks out loud. But when Sam feels comfortable or is with his favorite person, he can talk on and on for hours on end.

Introverts find energy, nourishment, and refreshment by spending time alone or with one or two special people tops—*that is it!* They prefer to interact with the world internally by reflecting on their thoughts and ideas before sharing them with others. If they get their alone time, they'll be able to enjoy playing with other kids and are more willing to be cooperative. If they don't get it, they'll get surly and upset. Others may see them as withdrawn, moody, or even anti-social, because small talk and participating all day long in school activities really tires them out.

Children with this persuasion tend to form deep and ever-lasting relationships with just a handful of people. Don't expect your child to come home every day with ten new friends after school. Less is more. As author Ayn Rand, an introvert, says about her upbringing, "My big clashes with Mother in childhood were [due to] the fact that I was anti-social, as she would call it. She always demanded that I be more interested in other children. Why didn't I like to play with others? Why didn't I have any girl-friends? That was kind of a nagging refrain."

Organizing Your Introverted Child

- Start by creating a comfortable and soothing atmosphere where less is more. Keep clutter to a minimum, and be sure things are easy to retrieve. Let the child try to arrange things in a way that works for him or her, and give the child space to maintain the setup. This will be an enormous ego boost and also a lot of fun for the child.
- When it comes to organizing, give your child time to unwind after school before you become demanding and insist that things get done. Allow them to think and process information before they have to respond and once they get going on organizing their notebooks and getting ready to do their homework. And above all, avoid interrupting them.
- Your introvert has a strong desire for personal space and personal reflection. They need peace and quiet to conquer anything. They are not anti-social but can find new situations and many people to be very draining and even toxic. Let other

members in the family know this as well as their teachers and close friends.

- Appreciate your introvert's observation skills, as they often receive fewer acknowledgments for who they are than does the highly socialized extrovert. Give them feedback in private, when they have time to be still and not upset if other people are around.

- Learn to be a good listener, and when they are ready to share, be sure you dedicate the time to be there for them.

- Introverts are challenged being with too many people or doing unexpected and unusual things. They tend to watch and listen before joining in a task that is new to them. When it comes to organizing, allow them to watch you, and sooner or later they will pitch in!

- They have an incredible ability to focus and concentrate and can become very involved in a project they are working on. Introverts tend to be thorough thinkers and want to take their time making decisions.

- They are also territorial about their space, especially their bedroom, and so if there is a "Keep Out" sign posted, honor it. Knock first and then request entrance.

- Sometimes it is a good idea to repeat a request or question you pose to your child more than once so they have time to think and then answer.

- Introverts may also be suspicious of compliments, uncomfortable with classroom participation, and terrified about standing in front of people. If you are scolding them, try not to make them the center of attention.

- They will feel devastated by having their physical space invaded to begin with and also prefer not to share personal stuff.

Tips for organizing your introverted child can initially be created by a comfortable and soothing atmosphere where less is more. Keeping things to a minimum and making things easy to retrieve is the key. Let them try to arrange things in a way that works for them and giving them space to maintain it. This will be an enormous ego boost for them and plus they will enjoy doing it.

Different children utilize their energy in different ways. It is really all about energy flow. The extroverted child gains energy when they are spending time with others, performing a task or interacting with the environment—quite the opposite for the introvert. They gain energy by thinking, pondering, working on a solo project, or interacting with just one or two other people. Introverts may even need to stop and rest just to replenish their energy source.

When parents gain energy in ways that are the opposite of their child's orientation, things can get sticky. An extroverted father recently said to me, "I can't believe my son and I drain each other." Dad needed to be more sensitive to his introverted son's needs. When he toned down his expectations and enthusiasm and gave his son a little more room to breathe, they found a new, happier place to be and play together. An introverted mother was having difficulties with her extroverted daughter. The mother had to tell her daughter that she can only attend a couple events a month or drive her to a couple lessons a week. That is simply how much the introverted mother could handle. She knows her limits yet is letting her daughter have freedom in her extracurricular activities.

CHAPTER 8

The Role of Gender

> Boys have slightly bigger brains, but there is no evidence that that makes them smarter. Girls' brains develop faster than boys' brains, but there is no evidence that that makes them smarter either.
> —David Walsh, *Why Do They Act That Way?*

In discussing gender differences, we must watch out for stereo-typical pink and blue ribbons to categorize the sexes. Just like brain types, one isn't better than the other, but there are definite outstanding genetic differences. Dr. Leonard Sax, author of *Why Gender Matters,* states that "We're not talking about small differ-ences between the sexes, with lots of overlap. We're talking about large differences between the sexes, with no overlap at all."

Boys' and girls' brains are wired in different ways and also grow in different directions. Viva la difference! For example, the left hemisphere of a girl's fetus brain develops before the right hemisphere. For boys, it is just the opposite; the right hemisphere develops first. The differences continue. The corpus callosum, the bridge of nerve fibers that unite the left and right hemispheres, are thicker in girls. That is probably what allows girls to multi-task/integrate/be social. Girls learn to do things like this much quicker than the boys do. Girls' brains are more adept at pro-cessing language skills, while boys' brains are more apt to excel at processing strategic skills. While boys tend to be more physically active in exploring their surroundings, girls tend to be less active and engage more in talking to one another.

The gender of our children defines and affects how we engage with them as well, and obviously, socialization issues affect how boys and girls learn and grow. Parents, for example, unconsciously spend more time with a child who is the same sex as they are. Parents also tend to talk to girls more than boys and might chastise boys more than girls. Parents also tend to give boys less freedom in determining what clothes to wear or how to decorate their rooms.

Let's explore gender differences to understand the unique ways we can get each child easily organized. Your child might not fit every generalized observation in this chapter—in fact, I'll bet he or she won't—but the broad outlines usually do apply, and there's much to learn if we tune in to the role of gender.

Girls

> Girls go to college to get more knowledge.
> Boys go to Jupiter to get more stupider.
> —Neil Howe, *Millennials Rising*

- *In early schooling, girls focus better on one activity than boys.*
- *Girls respond more to social stimuli.*
- *Girls do better on verbal tasks. Their brains are better organized for speech.*
- *Girls are more emphatic.*
- *Girls can recognize photos of their mother when they are only four months old; boys cannot until much later.*

- *Girls are more sensitive to the sound of people's voices.*
- *Girls are able to maintain eye contact longer.*
- *Girls talk earlier than boys.*
- *Girls tend to master reading and writing before boys.*
- *Girls often have an easier time finding things than boys.*

Girls' brains tend to develop faster than boys. They may lead boys in learning, can focus on problems a lot longer, and excel at school much earlier. Some girls also have a genetic knack to connect to people, faces, and voices. But Dr. Sax, author of *Why Gender Matters,* states that "while boys systematically overestimate their own ability, girls are more likely to underestimate their abilities." No surprises here. Girls tend to undervalue their talents, and obviously, one of our roles as parents is to support and encourage their self-esteem.

Helping Your Daughter Get Organized

- Some girls prefer someone around to support them when they do their homework, get packed for a trip, and get organized.
- Girls tend to like to engage in their own projects, but be ready to show up and stick around as you launch a new task. Your presence, even if you are just outside the room, will work wonders.
- Girls need landmarks in their room, closet, even purse. These guideposts help them know what's what and where. They need to know where they keep their glitter nail polish or their favorite nighttime book in their predictable space. Usually one thing's placement will trigger another one and so on and so on.
- Let's face it: girls are more likely to share their emotions, are

concerned with people and their feelings, and respond differently to discipline from boys. Girls need discipline, certainly, but it needs to be given in a softer, more gentle way. They don't do well with loud, authoritative directions. Instead, a warm and low-key approach can actually work well when setting up a structure and organizing a task.

- Talk them through the organizing problem first and ask for their input. Chances are, they will give it to you!
- Set a time limit to the task. Often girls can get carried away at explaining how they acquired something or talk too much on the phone while working away. Give them perimeters to getting things done.
- Most children get very little positive feedback, especially when it comes to the realm of organizing. Applaud her organizing brilliance!
- Reward her with some, not many, different kinds of organizing baskets. Girls tend to appreciate great-looking things! She will be happy to go shopping with you!

Boys

> In every real man, a child is hidden that wants
> to play.
>
> —Friedrich Nietzsche, *www.brainyquote.com*

- *Infant boys are much fussier than infant girls.*
- *The actual weight of the male brain is 15 percent greater than a female brain.*
- *Boys are better at moving around three-dimensional objects*

*and have more developed mental constructs of depth percep-
tion and spatial planning.*

- *Boys are more active and watchful than girls.*
- *Boys prefer activities that are more physical and require
  movement.*
- *Boys aren't bothered as much as girls are by other people's
  reactions or judgments.*
- *Boys are better at solving mazes.*
- *Boys often gravitate toward equipment.*
- *Boys respond more to things than to people.*
- *Boys understand relationships in the physical world better
  than girls.*
- *Boys are more often diagnosed with ADD than girls.*
- *Boys spend less time on an activity than girls.*
- *Boys take longer to process feelings than girls.*

As Maria Montessori said, "Think of a young boy in his first years
of life as a 'spiritual embryo.' " Young boys, in some ways, are so
unaware or naïve of what is going on around them. Girls have a
much better sense of things. They are slower to develop the so-
cial/emotional connections and can be even more sensitive to
girls at this early stage. By and large, boys have a harder time interacting and being social at home and in school. The traditional
educational system tends to be gender-blind and certainly doesn't
know quite how to support boys to interact with more ease and
fun. Even in kindergarten, the classroom tends to be organized
with more emphasis on the verbal than the physical. Thus boys,
who are less verbal than girls (it took Einstein five years to speak)
and more spatially oriented are at a double disadvantage.

Boys seem to be more judging than girls, meaning they are

less likely to accept the status quo around them without question. Recent studies mention that boys who are officially diagnosed with attention deficit disorder (and the percentages of boys over girls with this diagnosis is huge) might actually not hear the teacher. Some boys are less auditory than girls but also are often more visual, and so they aren't necessarily ADD but may be just bored.

Helping Your Son Get Organized

- Give him a goal list, and let him decide which one should be done first.
- Try giving him a specific list of what you want him to get done (pick up everything off the bedroom floor, organize your books, empty the garbage can).
- Give him a written chart of directions of things to do. They get jazzed up, on fire, and full of possibilities when they *see* the steps ahead of them. They enjoy checking off the list and celebrating their accomplishments. Boys respond to appropriate expectations and clear instructions.
- Spend a little time with them and let them solve their organizing problems.
- When you help your boy child get organized, don't be surprised if he wants to give you the orders about how to go about it. He may not appear open to listening to your new ways of doing things. Sound familiar?
- To help him keep track of his homework first, make his backpack easy for him to get things in and out of (buy a new bag with few pockets). Second, give him a place to easily throw things into when he gets home (a big basket at the entrance).

Third, duplicate the same books at home and at school (if he is always forgetting them). Fourth, let him do his homework in a number of places in the house (by having his schoolwork supplies in a rolling cart that could move around with him). Lastly, create a "Homework Completion Page" where the parent or baby-sitter has to have him sign-in before dinnertime.

- Make it really easy for them. Keep it all very simple with minimal instructions.
- Let them take the lead, if possible. It is important to let boys have independence and feel like they are in charge. Let them discover and claim these ideas for their own while making sure they are supported and applauded for their leadership on the task at hand. Only assist if necessary.
- Let him get into the physical experience of getting organized. Let him go to the garage to get containers, take the garbage out of what he has purged, and move his things around.
- Once you get their attention, have all the supplies ready. Now that they are finally ready, don't waste the moment.
- Boys are also master space planners. They can throw images around in their heads and in moments out it comes. Arranging furniture in the house or restacking boxes in the garage are simple solutions they love to come up with.
- By the ages of seven or eight, he should be allowed to choose the posters on his walls, the screen saver on his computer, and what kind of clothing to wear.
- Give him a reward when he completes a task.

CHAPTER 9

Organizing in a Zoo:
How the Different "Animals" in Your Family Can Thrive Together

> Blessed is the flexible parent, for he or she will have the greatest opportunity to communicate with his or her child.
> —H. Norman Wright, *How to Talk So Your Kids Will Listen*

As the complexities of modern life increase and time seems to decrease, every parent shares in the struggle to keep his or her family living, loving, and working together. This challenge becomes even more extreme when you throw into the already-rich mix the typical dramatic changes that happen in our personal lives. Add a new baby, a divorce, a change of neighborhood, or an illness, and the struggle to be a happy, healthy family becomes even more difficult. As author David Elkind describes in his book, *All Grown Up and No Place to Go,* "Today's child has become the unwilling, unintended victim of overwhelming stress—the stress borne of rapid, bewildering social change and constantly rising expectations."

In my experience as a professional organizer, I know that few homes have a working structure to accommodate the turmoil and chaos of daily life. Many children who inhabit two homes (with divorced parents) must deal either with parents who are often rigid and rule-bound or those who are hugely permissive, with few rules. Running a blended household, trying to solve a myriad of organizing dilemmas, and experiencing financial and lifestyle changes can make coming up with organizing solutions a real challenge.

When faced with new rules and situations, children often feel challenged and put off balance. Sometimes they can even experience momentary changes in their health and behavior. There is a lot of stress for children who have two different homes, inconsistent parenting, single parents, four parents, or both parents working. Nowadays, 5.4 million kids live with their grandparents.

Household To-Do's for Everyone

> If you take it out, put it back.
> If you carry it in, carry it out.
> If you borrow it, return it.
> If you open it, close it.
> If you throw it down, pick it up.
> If you take if off, hang it up.
> If you break it, fix it.
>
> —Donna Smallin, *Organizing Plain and Simple*

There are some basic guidelines to follow when it comes to getting adults and children to keep their shared environment organized and functional:

- Give your time. Kids need more of your time instead of more stuff.
- Be flexible. Home rules are evolving and changing, but be consistent.

- Have a "Job Jar." Write down every domestic duty on slips of paper. Drop these in the jar and let the kids pull them out at random. This prevents favoritism.
- Organize a monthly household clean-it-up day.
- Hold family meetings. Address the rules and rewards to be sure everyone knows what is what.
- Encourage mutual respect. Speaking disrespectful is off-limits.
- Put together one master phone list for adults' and children's important numbers.
- Maintain a daily schedule of household duties. Indicate who does what when.
- Make the last Sunday of the month organizing day, and choose at least one area of the house to be decluttered.
- Ask. Don't demand.
- Allow time for teaching and practicing organizing tasks.
- Don't take your kids' behavior personally, but do enforce direct consequences if they act out.
- Be mindful of any changes or transitions your kids are going through. They can adapt but need to always feel safe in the process.

If Your Child Has Two Homes

- Try to develop similar routines at both homes.
- Provide the child with his or her own space, at the very least a special closet and set of drawers just for them. If possible, in his or her own room.
- Avoid contradicting your spouse. All spouses need to be on the same page when it comes to home rules, expectations, rewards, and consequences.

- If your kids spend time in two homes, write up a packing list that includes personal belongings and school stuff. Double up supplies. Personal toiletries and school supplies should exist in both places.
- Allow them to do much of their own packing and unpacking.

The Multi-Thinking-Style Family

> If there is anything that we wish to change in the child, we should first examine it and see whether it is not something that could better be changed in ourselves.
>
> —Carl Jung, *The Integration of the Personality—*
> *Bartlett's Familiar Quotations*

Learning how to communicate with different thinking styles and creating diverse lifestyle resolutions is an enormous challenge—and a worthwhile one. As you learn to practice and apply the strategies in this book, you will discover that everyone can work and live together quite successfully. Kids will feel more confident, and the entire family will thrive with a secure feeling of well-being and enjoyment. No matter how chaotic everything appears now and then, all of you will have the skills and understanding to make it all work.

Now it's time to find out more about how to improve and enhance your interactions with your child. Knowing your own thinking style is key. If you can easily identify yourself from the quizzes and descriptions in this book, great. If not, or if you'd like more information on adults' thinking styles, please refer to my previous book, *Organizing for Your Brain Type.*

The next section addresses all the numerous ways you can communicate with and organize your child. There are different approaches for getting them ready for bed, getting their homework done, and getting them to school on time. Differences can become difficulties if they are not understood. Different parents, siblings, and teachers all can contribute to even more stress and confusion. So parents, you are about to be enlightened to ways in which you can get the organizing message out there to your children that will be understood, embraced, employed, and maintained. Your job is important, as your children will ultimately imitate what you do. If you are able to put your needs aside and really focus on what works for them, you will be happy and they will be happy. Working and living together in ways that honor all our innate gifts as well as support all our passions is the message behind this chapter.

The Maintaining-Style Parent—"Precision"

> You cannot teach a man anything; you can
> only help him find it within himself.
> —Galileo Galilei, *www.rit.edu*

Let's face it: as a Maintaining-style parent, you are probably one of the most hardworking, productive, competent, and reliable people out there. You really want to make every situation work, and you'll do everything you can to accomplish each and every task. With the children, you tend to be patient and forgiving. You prefer to avoid conflicts at all costs. You are also generous, cooperative, and willing to help in all situations. Maintainers love having everything done on time or before and take pride in delivering all projects in tip-top shape. Obviously, you take organizing very seriously as well. You even like it! Unfortunately, you may be the only one in the family who relishes cleaning out the refrigerator. The three other thinking styles may appreciate your help although they may fail to validate you for all you do.

People may find you rigid and somewhat inflexible. Oops, but doesn't someone have to keep things in order? Sure, you have a strong need for things to be just perfect, and you relish being in charge of every aspect of your environment. But sometimes your family members see you as unwilling to bend to suit their thinking styles. However, you ultimately need a sense of solid stability and routine to feel good. When you request the other three thinking styles honor your organized, precise style, you might be construed as having little sense of humor. You might even be called boring, no fun, or a stick in the mud. I assure you, you are the master organizer, but that doesn't mean people kick up their heels at the sight of a well-stacked bookshelf!

Let's explore how you can respect and work with your non-Maintaining-style children so you do not get in their way and yet remain intact and validated for what you do. Here is a summary of personality and thinking traits to help you get to know yourself better. Once you appreciate your own talents and individuality, you will be able to get out of your own way a little to focus on understanding and meeting your child's particular needs.

The Maintaining-Style Parent:

- You expect people to honor your word.
- You need structured group events to make new friends.
- You are very private and aren't willing to share that much with other people.
- You enjoy getting and staying organized. Everything has a place.
- You move slowly, not like the rest, especially the Innovator and the Prioritizer.
- If you need to adapt to a situation that isn't working, give yourself some time and tell yourself that it is just a little different from what you normally have done in the past. Be patient with change.
- You may need your own private space in your home. Create at least one area that is in total order that makes you feel good.
- You value past experiences and events.
- You are not impulsive and won't do or buy anything without thinking it out.
- Don't get stuck doing all the household duties by yourself if it doesn't match your standards. You are teaching skills, remember.
- You like to plan out all your events and schedules in advance. You like to predict what will happen.

Maintaining-Style Parent + Prioritizing-Style Child

Of all the three thinking styles, Maintaining parents and Prioritizing children tend to get along the best. Because both of your skills and natural talents are oriented in the left side of the brain,

I have found the best way to give advice to
your children is to find out what they want
and then advise them to do it.

—Harry S. Truman, *www.wisdomquotes.com*

Maintainers and Prioritizers tend to agree on the basics. You both demand excellence, strive for perfection, and appreciate beautiful and neat appearances. No silly chitchat for either of you two. Maintainers and Prioritizers mean business. When you want to bake a birthday cake together, for example, it gets done and looks and tastes fantastic. You are both serious and willing to take responsibility for your actions. However, chances are that you, Maintainer parent, are the one who keeps things in order and does a lot of the things your Prioritizing child doesn't want to do. But you don't mind because your child will usually verbalize his or her appreciation and will always give you the space to help them out.

Here's a little anecdote that illustrates how your two thinking styles, which appear quite different on the surface, are actually highly compatible. You, Maintainer parent, are playing Dogopoly (Monopoly for dog lovers), with your Prioritizer child. You're both taking the game very seriously. He is determined to win at all costs. Chances are, you are the banker, using your logical thinking cap and gifted organizing skills to keep everything in line. Your child, on the other hand, expresses forthright self-confidence and huge determination to break the bank. You both enjoy the game, don't waste any time, and value accurately tallying up the scores at the end. When the game is over, no tears are shed. You both innately agree, it's time to move on to the next thing.

Because you and the Prioritizing child both appreciate brief communications, you can take care of business and play with efficiency and zest. (Prioritizers dislike details and tend to go for shortcuts.) I know a couple siblings who exhibit a revealing dynamic. Carolyn, the Prioritizer, was merciless in achieving her goals at basketball. Her brother George, the Maintainer, consistently set her up with perfect passes, making sure his sister's bounced ball always landed in the same place. Carolyn learned and recognized the pattern and did her layouts with great success. Here's a great example of the Maintainer as the worker/support team and the Prioritizer as the leader. You and your child make a great team as well, but don't forget to stand up to your Prioritizer child, or you might be taken advantage of!

You speak the same language, so you can give them guidelines and the appropriate details that will ensure their goal planning and success. Like you, they, too, can play and work independently, but whereas you like to focus on the little details and have a concrete plan of attack, they tend to focus on not only the little things, but rather, on the big picture. If they want to go camping, you can get everything together and be ready for next assignment. They have a confidence that you can only dream of, but they need you to help them pull it all off. Because they trust you and value what you do, even though they may never say it, be sensitive to their ego and sense of pride. Your Prioritizer child just wants to be the "big man or woman in the house"—even though they are only eight years old! They need to feel important, and they need to be treated that way.

Prioritizers like to control things around them, and you may have to bite your lip not to offend their spirit. You truly give them comfort to make their goals manifest and know how important you are in contributing to their sense of self-assurance when they are about to make big decisions. However, be careful. Because by your very nature you are very unassuming, don't let them boss you around or intimidate or belittle you for what you do for them. Maintainers do so many important things for their home and workplace. If you feel disrespected or not appreciated by the Prioritizer, do come out and say it. If you respect what you do and who you are, so should they.

Pretend for a moment you and your Prioritizer child are both in school together. You would turn in neat, orderly assignments on time, all the time. You would also take your studies seriously and would be moved to challenge the teacher if you noticed errors in the assignment or in your textbooks. There would be no time for horseplay, and you would show little tolerance for doing anything out of order.

The Prioritizer, on the other hand, cannot handle predictability. They get bored when things are too routine, and because they are rarely shy, they speak out about how they believe things should happen differently. They actually enjoy being the leader and setting the tone, while you prefer being in the background.

When it comes to home life, the Maintainer parent likes to keep things in order. You preach, "Everything has a place and a place for everything." You always know what you are up to and live by a routine, even on the weekends. Prioritizers like that you are taking care of "their" stuff and will come up with brilliant arguments why you should continue. They are natural delegators, but because you both thrive on structure, you can handle knowing what you job is and take pride that your Prioritizer child appreciates it.

All in all, the Maintainer parent and the Prioritizer child share a similar gene to make everything work and work well. Naturally, you have different styles and approaches, but put you two together and you are sure to have success. As you learn to work together to control your surroundings and create a stable and structured world, you will enjoy how you complement one another more and more. You both can live, love, work, and organize well together as long as you the Maintainer parent take charge and don't get too resentful because of your dynamic and often too bossy Prioritizer child.

Maintaining-Style Parent + Innovating-Style Child

> There are only two lasting bequests we can
> hope to give our children. One is roots, the
> other, wings.
>
> —Hooding Carter, *www.wisdomquotes.com*

You both approach life and conquering the mundane from very different perspectives. The Innovator child is imaginative, creative, and unconventional. They are not into organizing much, let alone respecting traditional organizing modalities. You Maintaining parent, on the other hand, is totally realistic, objective, and approaches a task with a logical sequence of steps. The Innovator child goes with the flow of whatever is stimulating them at the time, hoping someone else (you) will pick up and finish whatever they leave hanging. You see, the Innovator has to blitz off to the next thrilling adventure. This child is certainly not lazy, but they are so turned on by each and every thing, they don't want to stop and finish something when they could dash off and begin something new. Never in a million years would you see them give up their originality for your love of form and structure.

Obviously, the Maintainer parent and the Innovator child require compromises to make their relationship work. You'll need to accept that they desperately need your help to solve problems and complete projects. But you'll be rewarded tenfold by their generous spirit, zest, and humor as you take care of the tasks at hand. Success will be found when you lighten up and they take a moment to pay attention!

Initially, you may have to loosen up your reins and not be so uptight or discouraged by your Innovator child. For example, they tend to make a lot of mistakes—though not purposefully, as they are running in a million different directions at once. They get bored with routine and prefer not to conform to existing structures. Don't expect them to come home every day from school and do their homework at the same time in the same place. Take a breath and relax. Your structured life is never going to work for them. Let them set their own work hours and locations—*as long as they do it.*

Let's begin with the challenge of organizing an Innovator child's bedroom. This is what you might hear them say: "I don't really care how things look." Or, "Mom, I know where everything is, so don't touch it." This kind of communication will drive you mad. Organizing for the Innovator child is terribly "relaxed." Be grateful for any kind of organizing they are willing to commit to, because to them, organizing is often unbearable. They dislike repetition, detailed procedures, and generic solutions, and on top of that, they are not very accurate. (Compare their organizing phobia to how you might feel if asked to do improv in front of a hundred people!)

Give your Innovator child a break! This may not sit well with you because you prefer to nitpick, sort, and put away every little thing. I assure you, it will be a waste of effort for you to complain, insist, or fuss. You will only be disappointed in their lack of taking responsibility. Don't think they are failures if they don't have everything in perfect order. They have other things, like singing, making art, dancing, to occupy their time, just as you have organizing duties that occupy your time.

In the midst of this seeming chaos, you can make a positive and helpful difference in their lives, but it requires communicating with them in a way that works. Try not to get angry or resentful. Don't feel pressured to lower your expectations, but know that the Innovator child is your opposite in so many ways. How they use their space and how they manage their time is going to be a challenge for you to understand and accept. But remember, it's not their problem, is it?

Lisa, a fourth-grade Innovator, claimed she knew where all her homework assignments were inside of her colorful binder, but every time she pulled out her notebook, her Maintainer mother winced. Mom couldn't understand how her daughter could keep track of her various subjects and project due dates because her stuff appeared to haphazard and messy. Lisa would plop down to do her homework, and all kinds of paper and notes seemed to scatter all over the table. Lisa drove her mom even crazier because of her seemingly chaotic behavior. One day Lisa did her homework on the floor, other days on the kitchen table, and even sometimes outside on the deck. There was absolutely no routine or consistency to her behavior. Ironically, it didn't cause that much trouble for Lisa, who was a solid B+ student. Mom was eager to enforce her perfect Maintaining style onto her daughter's loose Innovating style. She felt if her daughter just got organized she'd also get all As.

Sure, being organized is great—but the Innovator child isn't that interested, and on top of that, is challenged with details. They are big-picture thinkers with more on their minds than where they put their pencil last. Remember, Maintainer parent, in spite of your high standards about organizing, your primary concern is in understanding your child's unique thinking style first. Lisa's notebook may not look perfect enough for you, but it works well enough for her!

Another thing that irritated Lisa's mother was that her daughter was late most of the time. It was hard on both of them. I suggested that Mom get used to giving her daughter an extra fifteen minutes before every activity and then give her a good loud warning when it was time to go. Because Mom is a Maintainer, it was pretty easy for her to organize herself around the new system. Don't ever expect the Innovator child to drop everything and get on your schedule, though. They need to complete or process whatever they are doing before they just get up and go. With your continual support and supervision, they will appreciate your help and will feel respected, not pulled or prodded along—less stress all the way around!

How do you deal with your Innovator child without changing yourself too much? How can you open up your attitude to accept their unique ways? Because they welcome change and are bold risk takers, they really represent a very different attitude toward your love of routine and predictability. Where the Prioritizer child welcomes the benefits of routine, the Innovator child has no clue and thrives in the unknown and what is to come. Rather

than surrounding themselves with lots of things to feel connected with others like the Harmonizer, the Innovator child sur-
rounds themselves with a motley collection of odds and ends
they *might* use for one of their creative projects. Mind you, they
often don't know what it is for what . . . yet! Maintainer parent,
breathe and smile. The best way to welcome this whirlwind child
is to deeply appreciate your differences.

Innovators prefer things to be placed out in the open. You
don't. A compromise for both of you is to hang a curtain nearby
and voilà, you can easily hide everything with the swish of your
hand. When it comes to their art supplies, toys, you name it, the
same solution applies. Keep everything out in the open and easily
accessible. It not only helps your child remember what they have,
but it also encourages them to use it. Because you follow rules
and they break them, if you can keep their things easy to reach
and return, chances are they will honor the system. Well, some of
the time!

In many ways, you two have the potential to work well together and may even complement one another. You provide solid
support, and they provide the fire and spunk! Having looser expectations of how you define organizing and giving them freedom
while being open to trying new methods every now and then is
the ticket! The Innovator child will have a lot of ideas, but you
need to keep a watchful eye on the follow-through of how things
get done. And know that your child wants to contribute, too. Listen
to them, and learn and enjoy the fact that they are willing to try almost anything. Having reasonable expectations will make this experience more enjoyable, and your Innovator child's high energy,
flexibility, and delight in life just might rub off on you!

Maintaining-Style Parent
+ Harmonizing-Style Child

> Where did we ever get the crazy idea that in
> order to make children do better, first we have
> to make them feel worse? Think of the last
> time you felt humiliated or treated unfairly. Did
> you feel like cooperating or doing better?
>
> —Jane Nelson, *www.wisdomquotes.com*

You love organizing, and your child loves you! What a perfect relationship. The Harmonizer child tends to be the perfect team player, always willing to lend a hand. They like to maintain things, too, but they are less disciplined and structured than you. Both of you are big keepers of stuff. However, the Harmonizer is more relaxed than you and far more emotionally attached to their things, especially their memorabilia. Where you hang onto things to provide a utilitarian service, their stuff keeps memories alive and connects them to people and warm feelings.

Your job is to keep them on track, on time, and focused on the job at hand. Don't forget, giving the Harmonizer a compliment or two along the way really helps! They certainly won't resist you, like the Innovator child. Instead, your Harmonizer will be happy for your help and truly needs it, as well. For example, when it comes to being someplace on time, give them extra time to get ready, as you would with the Innovator, but stay physically close to your Harmonizer while they prepare. They like being near you and will probably work faster and get out the door earlier if you are close by. They are consistently running late, always at the whim and need of someone they care about whom they think needs them. Truth is, the Harmonizer child puts other people first.

This can be a tricky situation because you don't want your child to become too dependent on you. Be sure they assume some responsibility, and give them advance warnings to be responsible. Remember, they want to please, not disappoint you. How do you go about supporting and getting them organized in a way that is also easy on you? Because Harmonizers collect lots and lots of things, you'll need to have an annual purge. What do you do with a room full of stuff that means little to you but the world to them? Show some interest in their collections. It will make them feel more comfortable as they begin tossing bits and pieces into the trash! Remember, your Harmonizer child collects souvenirs and mementos because they are threads to happy places and happy times. They dislike being alone, so Harmonizers embrace their material objects, which bring them comfort and make them feel in harmony with their environment.

When you begin to purge, it is important that you recognize that the Harmonizer child has a short attention span, so do the cleanup process in bits, say once a month. It is important that you act like an intimate companion while they part with their possessions. If they sense your physical presence and approval, they will be more willing to let go. A+ for you if you can nurture and not scold them while going through a process that for you alone would be quite easy. Harmonizers thrive in a motivational environment, so keep cheerleading and give them lots of hugs. Ultimately, they will be glad you helped clear out their room for more things to come!

If you can create the structure for them to flourish and monitor them along the way, your Harmonizer child will be able to keep their things in line. Remember that it takes a long time for them to complete a task, and interruptions from the TV or the phone can derail any organizing gains they have made. Keeping them focused is a challenge. However, if they feel good about what they are doing because of your brilliant coaching, they will want to get it all done. As a result, they will develop self-confidence because they know their room is in order to entertain and just hang out in. Giving them time to work through this process, they can be comforted and grow into a loving person who respects others as well as themselves.

The Harmonizing child will get organized if he or she is in the right mood. Their pace at getting anything accomplished has to be cushioned around discussions, so break things up and re-energize them with chitchat. Or make them feel loved and happy by treating them to a pancake breakfast or an outing to the pumpkin patch before diving into the work at hand.

Lastly, you, the Maintainer parent, really thrive in an environment where you are in control. As caregivers, you set very high standards and can be seen as being too critical, strict, or too much of a perfectionist. You provide an enormous sense of security and a safety net for your family. You are very family-oriented and loyal, but pick your organizing battles. You may not win everyone over to your style, and things may not go quite your way, but don't forget that people value and respect you. Even though you prefer things be done right or not at all, people in your life have a hard time meeting your perpetually stiff standards. Unless you live with a household of other Maintainers, your demands may alienate you from your family. Therefore, don't expect others to value things you value. Most people don't do well on a tight, restrictive schedule 24/7.

I have a client, Jim, whose father, a Maintainer, set impossibly high standards. Even when Jim was mowing the lawn, his father found fault, constantly criticizing and correcting him. Unfortunately, this kind of perfectionism took its toll on Jim, who to this day claims he hates to garden. Try not being so intense, as unhealthy perfectionism can make children feel insecure, unworthy, and unhappy.

Lastly, don't avoid conflicts by walking away and reorganizing the pantry one more time. Open up and try to verbalize your feelings. Remember, the order in the house can wait while you build good, healthy, happy relationships.

The Harmonizing-Style Parent—"People First"

> Give a little love to a child, and you will get a
> great deal back.
>> —John Ruskin, *The Crown of Wild Olive 1*—
>> *Bartlett's Familiar Quotations*

Organizing is a bit of a challenge for you because as a Harmonizer, you value connecting with people and making sure everyone is happy much more than doing chores or arranging the garage! You place a high value on loyalty, honesty, and friendships of every kind. You also enjoy rituals, parties, and get-togethers and rarely miss an opportunity to celebrate a dear friend or family member's birthday or graduation. Along the way, you end up collecting and cherishing all kinds of keepsakes, mementos, and odds and ends at an almost alarming rate. These things aren't simply objects to you; they elicit special feelings, warm memories, and happy times.

Your optimism runs high, but so does your need for approval. You crave acceptance and are a people-pleaser. If you aren't careful, you sometimes lose your own ground. Pulled in different directions by the desires of others, you may give up fulfilling your own needs first and then can lose some important self-respect. When it comes to organizing, Harmonizers are the thinking style most tuned in to their emotions and the feelings of others. Sometimes Prioritizers, Innovators, and Maintainers will find you too emotional, too personal, or too interruptive. How can you remain true to yourself and yet be helpful to those around you, particularly your children?

The Harmonizing-Style Parent:

- You give so much to everyone else. Honor what you enjoy, and make an effort to do it as often as possible.
- You like physical connections with people. Be sure you create a comfortable and welcoming home.
- You can honor all your special things by having less of them. Keep your memorabilia on display in your room and not stored in your attic.
- Honor your sensitivity, and let others know that noise, and even a tone of voice, can upset you.
- Organize slowly. Most of your stuff has a lot of meaning and personal value, so take your time sorting.
- Set healthy limits in your life so you don't spend all your time helping others.
- Indulge and enjoy celebrating and giving parties for all kinds of occasions.
- You love a beautiful environment. Give yourself permission to create a place that nourishes your soul.

Harmonizing-Style Parent
+ Maintaining-Style Child

> People's behavior makes sense if you think
> about it in terms of their goals, needs, and
> motives.
>
> —Thomas Mann, *www.rit.edu*

The Harmonizing parent can feel a bit hurt or even offended by the seemingly standoffish Maintainer child. These children tend to be more conservative in their behavior and certainly less emotionally expressive than you. Maintainers value consistency and routine over people and feelings. They are probably not too concerned about your thoughts or emotional state and would rather have you be efficient in your actions than talkative or overtly huggy or kissy. Maintainers basically want to get to work and without interruption until they are done with the task at hand. However, for you, feelings are much more important than checking things off a to-do list.

The Maintainer child wants to be left alone until they decide they are ready to engage. Whereas you value people, they value time. They prefer quiet and want to solve their problems on their own. If you need to correct them or guide them in any way, it is best to change your typical style. Act a tad more serious, get to the point, and then leave the room. Try not to feel hurt by their seemingly distant behavior. They do love you, but they are far more reserved than you and rarely wear their heart on their sleeve.

As their caregiver, it is your job to make the best out of the situation and align your skills and insight to their organizing game plan. Give your Maintainer child precise instructions; stick to the subject at hand, and then respectfully let them figure it out. You will get so much out of working with their meticulous talents instead of fighting the river. If you can bear to do it, write down all your requests on a chalkboard and hand it to them or post a clear list of things to do on their bedroom door. Feel a little stifled? Don't worry; they will respond so well to your careful approach that you'll find everything is better organized and works more efficiently. They are great helpers and are more than willing to do anything you wish as long as they know well beforehand where they are going and what is expected of them.

You both operate at different tempos. You tend to move much slower and need to be tantalized to get off and running. Not them! They are already on task while you sigh and gaze through your rose-colored glasses. To respect their desire to have things in order and structured, you may have to step up to their organized plate and at least cheerlead them on. Be sure you keep things fun and upbeat, and don't ever take their behavior too personally. If you can open yourself up to being supportive instead of being thwarted by your Maintainer child's style, you will be amazed at the gifts they bring. Yes, your Maintainer child will teach you, the Harmonizing parent, how to get and stay organized!

Maintaining styles know they are talented in this department. If you show them that you respect and value organizing— well let's not take this too far. If you show them you are willing to try to focus, they will appreciate it. What excites the Maintaining style are good manners, clear guidelines and expectations, and being able to accomplish a task. For you to pull off this blitz, be sure you take some short breaks, call a friend, put on some music, and take a breath of fresh air. This can be a real win-win relationship if you nurture your Harmonizer needs along the way.

Lastly, don't let your Maintainer child make you feel less because you aren't a fastidious folder of shirts or a precise labeler of jars. Admit that your child can't help, but raise the organizing bar and celebrate their skill set. Being the warm, empathetic person you are, applaud, delight, and make it work at all costs. Don't be threatened by their competency and demands for perfection. You measure up quite nicely on your own.

Harmonizing-Style Parent + Prioritizing-Style Child

> Train up a child in the way he should go and
> when he is old, he will not depart from it.
> —Proverbs 22:6

If the Maintaining child intimidates you, the Prioritizing child will prove to be even more of a handful! You are polar opposites in so many ways. They want approval and success, as you want companionship and peace. Because the Prioritizer child wants to be the leader, let them initiate conversations, make decisions, and take some risks. Don't challenge them, but remember, as a parent, you have the final say.

They can be your nemesis on all fronts, so be sure you let them "magically" control the organizing process. Prioritizers are completely task-centered and extremely hardworking. No matter the obstacles, they will spend the necessary time and effort to get it all done! They love results, but Prioritizers resist taking little steps and aren't in love with to-do lists. You might have to pick up the detail slack, not your favorite assignment, but you better than them!

If you have a young Prioritizer child, it can be difficult to let them take the lead and control the situation. However, you can do numerous things to inspire them to want to get organized in the first place. Remember, they are much more interested in delegating tasks to you, their younger siblings, and whoever else is around. You see, they just don't feel they have time to do the nitty-gritty because they are always thinking about their next conquest, like who is going to win the ball game tonight or who will get the best seat at the restaurant.

When it comes to organizing their room, giving a Prioritizer orders never works. However, if you give them logical guidelines and a brief agenda and set realistic goals, they will take great pride in getting things done in ship-shape order. Out of all the thinking styles, Prioritizers tend to work fast and furious, compared to your much slower, relaxed manner. If you can help them feel important and give them some accolades when they are done, they are more than likely to repeat their efforts time and time again.

How can you accommodate your thinking style and support the Prioritizer in your life at the same time? Sometimes they can cut you off and move forward while stepping on your toes, without much sensitivity or understanding. Don't let their assertiveness belittle or humiliate you. They are just not as sensitive as you are. Try not to complain around them, and don't appear to waste their time. They'll be even more curt. If they are being difficult, don't be difficult back. Fighting with them is just too much for a Harmonizer like you. Plus, they excel at debate and they'll win. Back off and return when you feel stronger and happier. Although you love to nurture and be supportive, the Prioritizer will challenge you to be strong and more forthright in your undertakings. It's an opportunity for you to work faster, be bolder, and be in control. Why not give it a try? And remember, if you can give them an abundance of ego boosts along the organizing road, they will work nonstop and solve all your organizing problems.

If you aren't threatened or offended by their competitive spirit and workaholic approach, you will find your Prioritizing child works miracles and gets an inordinate amount done. Because they manage their space and time effectively, they will use every tool and every form of assistance they can to emerge triumphantly in all they do. They ultimately want power, to be in control, and to win. If you can support your child in a way that encourages their confidence and take-charge attitude, you will guarantee a great life for them on all fronts.

Harmonizing-Style Parent + Innovating-Style Child

> Come forth into the light of things, let nature
> be your teacher.
>
> —William Wordsworth, *www.rit.edu*

Living with an Innovator child isn't as difficult as being with the Prioritizer but not as easy as the Maintainer. Innovators are happy to work alone, like the other two thinking styles, but they also enjoy some company—as long as you make them laugh! However, the Harmonizer/Innovator combo presents an impulsive duo—two minds that really would rather do anything but organize! You are both highly social creatures and can adapt to almost every situation. Because neither of you are terribly motivated by deadlines or external realities, you can have a lot of fun and laughs together, and hopefully organize somewhere along the way.

The Innovator child might see you as a tad dependent, and you might see them as a bit of a rebel rouser, but a real enjoyment of life bonds you two at a deep level. Both you and your Innovator child have issues with time. The Innovator can lose all sense of time, and lost in their creative juices might forget there is a deadline or a time constraint. You as a Harmonizer can also be easily distracted, but at least you have the ability to know when activities begin and end. The Innovator child rarely has a clue, and they depend on you to remind them what's happening when. They are either on or off. Don't fight it; you can't win. Instead, try to lovingly tune in to their natural biorhythms and in no time you will learn how to help them help you help them!

Innovators tend to be careless, and when it comes to taking responsibility, they would rather not have any. Because you are a natural cheerleader, you can easily support and encourage their concerns without suppressing their creativity and passion. Your child will learn to trust you and will count on you to help them focus and take care of things that are important to them.

When it comes to organizing, if your Innovator knows there is fun up ahead, they are sure to join in. Approach the task at hand in a casual manner, but maintain an open, forgiving heart. You never know what will come out of their mouths, so don't take their words personally! And pay attention to them. They love to goof around, and you never know when they might become so totally absorbed that they sleep at their desk all night long or get so bored they simply wander away.

A Harmonizer parent needs to approach their Innovator child in a playful manner. Don't let them see you as heavy-handed, helpless, or needy. That will turn them right off from you and organizing. Their imagination feeds them, and if you can make organizing an exercise in creativity and discovery, without a serious overtone, they will be all over it!

At home, you both can have so much fun because you are connected to art, entertainment, and invention. Innovators love experimentation. You can do them a great service by giving them all kinds of new strategies for organizing their rooms. Avoid being boring at all costs, and you'll always be invited into their wacky bedroom, filled with a smorgasbord of stuff, all left out in the open, so they can pick up whatever they feel moved to use for a dramatic moment or a drawing assignment. Harmonizers like to see things everywhere, too, so your Innovator's room probably doesn't make you terribly nervous. As you learn to delight in their constant flow of ideas and share some of their energy and passion, you'll find you are in for the ride of your life!

Lastly, the Harmonizer, you are the most optimistic and cooperative of all the thinking styles, and you would share the shirt off your back if it improved someone else's life. Your fun-loving parenting skills display affection and the desire to maintain an upbeat, happy, and comfortable home. You also are fed when other people acknowledge your contributions. This can be a challenging situation, as you don't want to alienate your children by disciplining them. Your number-one aim is to be liked. Because you take things personally and are rarely competitive, you tend to give in to what members of your family want. Your parenting style may be a tad permissive, as you aren't that consistent enforcing the rule, and you communicate more on an emotional than rational level. Your kindness and generous spirit needs some balance, so try not to let others boss you around and take advantage of your good nature.

Organizing for you can be a bit of a challenge, as you value people and are concerned with their well-being much more than all your stuff. Your positive, cheerleading qualities go a long way adapting and learning new approaches to getting organized. Because you celebrate almost every occasion, never missing the opportunity to let someone know how much you appreciate them and value who they are in the world, you tend to gather things at an alarming rate. Because you make most of your decisions based on your mood and give validity to your many emotional needs, you look for loyalty and honesty in all friendships.

Your optimism runs high, however, and so does your need for approval. Being motivated for social recognition, you need others to accept you much of the time. People's needs drive you and motivate you to act. Be careful not to fall off the boat, as you are likely to be pulled in many different directions by the needs of the other three thinking styles. You can still be kind, but do be sure your happiness is part of the overall situation.

When it comes to organizing, you have learned that there are four distinct ways that motivate people. All the others don't have a great access to their emotional needs, and are, therefore, going to find you to be too emotional, too personal, and too interruptive. How can you remain true to yourself yet helpful to those around you?

The Innovating-Style Parent—"Possibility"

You are a master of originality, wit, and high adventure. Nothing can get in the way of your passion. Your persistence, imagination, and creativity rule the roost. You probably have great times with your family and friends because of your playful personality. You

> Children need guidance and sympathy far
> more than instruction.
>
> —Anne Sullivan, *www.wisdomquotes.com*

are curious and eager to try new methods for everything, even organizing! When it comes to parenting, you are willing to adapt to the unexpected and delight in coming up with new solutions. If you fail at something, who cares? Next time you will come back in spades and dive into the problem with just as much enthusiasm.

You are truly an optimist and always see the good in everyone and everything. Because you have endless amounts of energy, you work passionately and quickly. Of course, sometimes you are a tad hasty and make a few mistakes, but so what? Find a Prioritizer or a Maintainer and have them organize the details. Keep yourself free to do what you do best—create and explore.

The Innovative-Style Parent
- Taking care of mundane details isn't your strong point. Get help. No need to go crazy.
- You get bored easily. Keep enough things around to stimulate your many interests.
- You thrive on new things, new ideas, and new people. Don't get bogged down in routine.
- You prefer working and creating alone. Be sure you have your own private nook.
- You only organize once in a blue moon. Once a year may be your limit!
- You are spontaneous and impulsive. Find others to steady you when you feel out of kilter.

- You love to begin projects. Get help when it comes time for completion.
- When you are upset, you tend to withdraw. Let friends and family know your behavior. It's a good way to not insult them and honor you at the same time.
- Be sure you have enough space to create. Get messy and unruly and have fun.

Innovating-Style Parent + Harmonizing-Style Child

> The job of the educator is to teach students to
> see the vitality in themselves.
> —Joseph Campbell, *www.rit.edu*

You and your Harmonizer child do pretty well together. That's because you actually have a lot in common. You both approach life with a lot of delight. Your Harmonizer child is loaded with warmth and personality, and you are the impulsive clown and adventurer. What a great duo! Both of you are willing to try new things without a lot of preplanning or fuss. Together you throw a memorable and lively celebration for friends and family, and you both can party long and hard. Even though you tend to be demanding, and unlike the Harmonizer, put creative solutions ahead of people and their needs, you bring focus to your Harmonizer child. Together you are unstoppable. All you need to do is be sure your Harmonizer feels they are an integral part of your world, and they'll be there at your side forever loyal and giving.

You both have deep connections to your possessions. You, Innovator, tend to link up with future ideas and what might come from your next big plan. The Harmonizer child is attached to the past and cherishes warm and fuzzy memories and memorabilia of good times. Together you are able to extrapolate a lot of creativity and meaning from what you own.

You two, fortunately, have similar takes on organizing, which come down to, "Can we both do something, anything else?" Your Harmonizer child will not criticize your "relaxed" manner of keeping things "together." Because the Harmonizer is very helpful and generous, they'll just want to be supportive as you invent new ways to stack your books and arrange the furniture. No matter how optimistic you are, it's time to face facts. The Innovator parent and the Harmonizer child kind of resemble "the blind leading the blind" when it comes to organizing. What to do? First of all, you need to come up with a deadline for all your organizing tasks. Let the Harmonizer watch the clock, and before you know it, you can party together when you are done.

Remember, Harmonizers are sensitive—far more than you are—and any attack or off-the-cuff remark can deeply affect them. Sometimes you think so quickly that you fail to realize what you said until after you said it. Be gentle and encourage them to get their room cleaned up without urgency or pressure. Your Harmonizer child needs to be told what to do and, in a friendly and positive manner, complimented along the way. When your soft words sink in, the Harmonizer child will be more than willing to please you. You see they want to make you happy! Set the stage, give them some easy directions, and let them take their time. Be sure you pop in and out to check on them. They like it when you are physically around. Don't worry; this can be a fun and successful organizing relationship if you find time to dance, sing, and laugh along the way.

Innovating-Style Parent + Maintaining-Style Child

> Opposites are not contradictory but complementary.
>
> —Niels Bohr, *www.rit.edu*

This is not a match made in heaven. You are both so different, especially in the realm of organizing. Your Maintainer child thrives with structure, moment-to-moment planning, and routines. That kind of behavior drives you crazy and ultimately depletes you. The Maintainer needs consistency and security. They crave routines and schedules, while you prefer lots of variety and unpredictability. Maintainers naturally plot out every day, usually on a calendar of some sort, often planning it down to the minute. You, on the other hand, frequently have no idea what you are doing tomorrow—and like it that way! As an Innovator parent, you also tend to be free-flowing and rather relaxed about how things might turn out. The Maintainer child tends to be a tad inflexible and worries about almost everything! Working and living with them is a challenge, but as long as you have realistic expectations about what they are willing and not willing to do, you will have a pretty good relationship.

Luckily, both of you are hard workers, and even though they tend to work a little slower than you, once they know the reasons why things need to be done, your Maintainer child will gladly pick up their pace and take care of business. If you can lay out a written outline for what I call "planned change," your Maintainer child will thrive. It gives them a built-in safety net of knowing what comes next and helps them feel secure. Perhaps it is a good idea to dampen your wild spirit a little bit when organizing with your Maintainer. They tend to be rather serious and don't want to feel mocked as they earnestly forge ahead.

As an Innovator, you welcome change, and as a result, you give your children tons of freedom. With the Maintaining style, this can get tricky, because it is rare for them to experience any spontaneity. They are not going to come up with some new, amazing ideas, so don't waste your time thinking they will. If you want them to deviate from the norm, give them explanations and clarify what you are doing before you actually do it. Don't be surprised if they analyze your ideas to death, and try to love them even when they just won't crack a smile.

Don't think they are being critical or difficult. Rather, the Maintainer child only feels safe and secure when everything is in order. This may go against your spontaneity and who you are, but this relationship asks you to expand beyond your thinking style. Learning to give and take and putting others people's feelings first might be a wonderful new practice for you.

Keep in mind that your Maintainer child expects perfection and perhaps, if you can get things started with your whirlwind energy, they can come in at the end and complete it, mistake free. Because they don't easily display emotions, the way they connect with their parents, siblings, and friends is to keep things in order, always tidying up their room and making sure their homework is done. They relish consistency and uniformity, and anything you can do to augment their success in that area will make them feel confident and happy.

If you are able to honor your child's thinking style, you will be well rewarded. Your Maintainer child will always support you to get organized and stay organized! They would like nothing better than to schedule an organizing session with you each and every week. This kind of "fun" activity comes naturally to them, and although it may start off a little painful for you, eventually you might end up enjoying it. It's one of the only ways to really bond with your fastidious child.

You should know that they are insecure and don't like to be made a fool of. Your sense of humor may need to be toned down a bit. They do want to please you but will feel stressed out if they are always waiting for you and will get quite upset if they gave you a paper to sign for school and you can't find it. So please, Innovator parent, try to be a little more conscientious. For example, create a regular place to file your daughter's school letters. Find a colorful box, and put it out on your desk! No biggie. Consider that a great first step! Luckily for you, if your child is of this persuasion, they will always finish what they start and perform everything in a very logical, methodical sequence. It is your job to provide them with the safety and space to express their need for order and regularity. Anything you can do to support their basic needs will ensure their success. They are only waiting for you to inspire them and then they can do all the rest.

Innovating-Style Parent + Prioritizing-Style Child

Let me start off by saying that you two are both big-picture thinkers who really don't like doing a lot of menial, nitpicky work. Because you both tend to work fast, move fast, enjoy change, and are major risk-takers, you could use a meticulous Maintainer

We can't form our children on our own con-
cepts; we must take them and love them as
God gives them to us.

—Johann Wolfgang Von Goethe,
Hermann and Dorothea

to keep everything organized and in place. As the Innovator parent, you end up getting stuck with taking care of more of the details than you'd like. But you are kind of out of luck because your
Prioritizer child will refuse to handle anything beyond rapid-fire
decision-making and coming out on top.

Ironically, Prioritizers are capable of organizing and actually
value it, but because they have a deep need to feel in control of
everything all the time, they can't imagine doing the tedious upkeep. Your Prioritizer child likes to be seen as a leader. They tend
to take life more seriously than you and always like to think before they act. They appreciate when things are neat and sparse,
and everything is working in tiptop shape. If you can slow down
a tad, be clear, and think before you speak, they will be more
trusting in you and your ideas. They are incredibly practical, as
they like to have things at their fingertips and, like you, they are
independent and very hardworking.

One of the hardest things about working and living with the
Prioritizing style is that they are very controlling. You need to
have a game plan developed way in advance, one that allows
goals to be stated and a real deadline set in stone. They are more
than willing to work fast and hard to get the job done if they feel
they have to. As the Innovator parent, let them finish it up and
give them all the credit. (Because that doesn't really concern you.)
If you can give them the reins and provide them with clear-cut

choices, they will generally make the right decision and emerge triumphant.

You need to be their cheerleader. Chances are, this may be a fun role for you to play at least some of the time. If you can recognize their accomplishments and feed them adulation and compliments, they will feel positive and continue doing what you asked them to. They have a big ego and a sense of pride, and coaxing them to get things organized will be a trick only you can do.

Time for them is very important, so don't waste it. This has to be one of your biggest challenges, and if you mess up, they will gladly let you know. They will let you know what they want in a hurry, and don't be surprised when they boss you and everyone else around. They are independent thinkers and like to keep busy and make their own rules. Everything for them is a competition, and they are always on the move. Your Prioritizer child has the ability to be a little demanding and rude. They will often question or even insult authority and may express overt disapproval of their teachers, camp counselors, or anyone else who gets in their way.

Both of you are leaders in your own right. As their parent, take charge but give them lots of options. Come up with a well-written list of things that need to get done, and allow them to pick the ones they want to do and in what order. This way, they get to feel in control and you get the job done. Divvying up the duties will give you more energy and allow for some things to be accomplished in a way that isn't too painful for either of you.

Lastly, the nitty-gritty of parenting is tough for you because you don't care to enforce rules and regulations. Instead, you thrive on new, stimulating, creative, and fun activities. Organizing a home can be a creative challenge for you, but you more than the others can use the support and encouragement from all the brain styles. Spending the day according to what it says in your day planner is a tricky assignment. You may ask, "Where is my day planner?" Keep everything simple, and be sure others know you need and appreciate their help.

The Prioritizing-Style Parent—"Progress"

If you bungle raising your children, I don't think whatever else you do well matters very much.

—Jacqueline Kennedy Onassis,
www.wisdomquotes.com

Out of the entire bunch of thinking styles, you tend to be the most demanding, goal-driven parent there is. Being strong-willed, tenacious, and hardworking, you want results now, not tomorrow. As a kid, you were probably a fearless, natural leader. You also intuitively knew how to set limits for you to act and meet your everyday challenges. You were usually successful at everything you tried and loved to win, win, win. Coming in first was your idea of a good time, all the time. You also are adept with language and enjoy employing your fancy verbal debating skills to convince others to do things you don't want to do.

You are big on speed, completing any project on time, and are driven by all your duties and tasks. Success is defined by how much you get done in a certain time frame and how you can come out on top. You have a remarkable work ethic that knows no boundaries. You need to be in charge, head of the household, and leader of the company as you provide a sense of security and decisive leadership to all that you know. You are the most dependable parent out there, a real rock of Gibraltar.

When it comes to organizing, you naturally prefer to keep very few things around. You like things to be done your way and hope you can train your family, your mate included, to do things you would rather not have to do. You are not a "team player" in the sense that you like to work independently and are always looking out for your needs to be met over anything else. You are a take-charge kind of person who demands a lot from yourself but also a lot from others.

Your work style is quick and efficient, and you hope others can come up to speed with you. You like having the possibility to shine and have public recognition in all that you do. You have little tolerance for indecisiveness, irresponsibility, or excuses from your family members. It's time for you to learn how to use new tools that will continue to help you get what you want but will also soften the edges of how you do what you do. That means you will keep winning, but not at the expense of hurting other people's feelings. Give it a shot! What have you got to lose?

The Prioritizing-Style Parent

- You don't like to deal with other people's feelings because you have bigger fish to fry.
- You are tough and get the job done. Don't make excuses for being bossy. You are the boss.
- You like to work nonstop and are always interested in furthering your career. You also make sure others have jobs and purpose along the way. A win-win.
- You are a little stingy and hate to waste things. So what?

- Honor the fact that you like things in perfect, functioning order.
- Your home is a place to relax and unwind. Be sure to get help organizing it to be just the way you like—spartan and aesthetically pleasing.
- You are smart and love a good debate. Don't push your power in everyone's face, but do stand your ground.

Prioritizing-Style Parent + Innovating-Style Child

> We must teach our children to dream with
> their eyes open.
>
> —Harry Edwards, *www.stresslesscountry.com*

Innovative kids can be a little challenge for you, but not as much as Harmonizing kids. Like you, they are big-picture thinkers and are excited by the possibilities of new ideas and directions, and they also enjoy challenges and conquests. Prioritizers are forceful, judgmental, and often controlling, but you must try to loosen up with your Innovator child. Don't expect them to meet your self-imposed deadlines, because they won't. Don't hover over them, supervising their every move, because they won't be able to function that way. The key word for you is "Relax!" It's foreign to your makeup but will serve you well. The next key word is "Lighten up." Your Innovator child is far less serious than you are, and rather than being driven by your desire to achieve recognition, they tend to do things by the sheer excitement and the pleasure of the experience. While you are calculated, they are free and easy.

I doubt you'll be able to bite your tongue and not lash out

when you delegate something to your Innovator and they either forget to do it or botch it up with a ton of mistakes. Sure, they work quickly, but they aren't that thorough. Being meticulous actually depletes them and makes them anxious. You don't have to lower your standards, but don't be too nitpicky, either. It is not that they are rude or reckless, it's just that they like to be absorbed into the pure fun of creating and aren't so stuck on the final results.

Although you are quite different, you are very important in their lives. You are able to help them get to events on time, keep track of their things, and stay on schedule. You may not like to be the one reminding them all the time, but you know that as Innovators, they can use all the help they can get. They do things when they feel like it and, as kids, don't really like any scheduled times for dinner or for going to bed. Chances are, they don't even have a clock in their room (or it's somewhere under the art books and ribbons) and rely on you to wake them up.

Because Innovators try anything once and may only do it again if they are prodded or see a remote benefit from it, they thrive for unexpected and unusual things. You may not be the best to lead them into this area, but you can certainly try to get out of their way. Give them their freedom, and let their imagination run wild as you control what will happen in the future and what needs to be cleaned up in the past. Remember, you are the leader and are good at knowing what works and what doesn't.

Chances are, if you become too narrow-minded and critique every move they make, they will feel confined and even angry. Try not to be too rigid, boring, or dull because you'll lose them. But if you can loosen up a little and open up to their innovative ways, you can expect a lot of fun, good laughs, and a whirlwind of wild adventures. Now and then accept their wacky dreams, and take a chance with them. You may be surprised how well you two relate when your strengths meet in the middle.

Prioritizing-Style Parent + Harmonizing-Style Child

> Parents wonder why the streams are bitter,
> when they themselves have poisoned the
> fountain.
>
> —John Locke, *www.josephsoninstitute.org*

This could possibly be a match made in heaven, as you are the true-blue leader and they are the devoted follower. Your Harmonizer child really enjoys doing the things you don't like to do. They aim to please, and much of their time is dedicated to making sure you are happy. If you express care and kindness to them, they will loyally do what you bid, but don't take advantage of them.

Harmonizing children normally like to play by other people's rules. If they feel engaged and part of something, they are more than willing to let someone else boss them around. How perfect for you! They will respect your authority and will not compete nor judge. Because they want to keep things in harmony, they may not have the most confidence and can be a little nervous. If would be great if a little of your strength and passion could rub off on them.

Prioritizer parent, be kind to your dear Harmonizer child. Never forget how much joy and comfort they give you. They enjoy spending time with you and are some of the most helpful and caring people around. If you are worried, they will give you solace. If you are lonesome, they will sit close by. When you want them to organize their bedroom, ask them to work slowly and don't demand that they get rid of what you think is way too much. They like to keep all their good memories and experiences around them. If you can be logical yet find a way to share heart-filled reasons why things need to be done a certain way, they will gladly respond in kind.

Don't expect your Harmonizer child to initiate any organizing goal on their own. They need prodding, coaching, and someone out there to be sure it all goes well. So be the leader you are, and know the more you are around while they are organizing, the better the outcome. Try not to tap your foot and gasp as you observe their turtle pace. Try not to interrupt them when they tell stories about this shell or that book that means so much to them. If you can show interest, even if you don't really get why they are so emotional about a matchbox, and are not threatening, they will do as they are told and will endear themselves to you in more ways than you can imagine.

It is important to them that they feel comfortable in their space, and again, remember, they need their things. A spartan Prioritizer's aesthetic isn't going to make them feel happy and safe. If their twenty-five stuffed animals piled all over the floor and bed look too messy for you in the morning, don't go into their room. Allow them to have their things in a way, within reason, to comfort them and make them feel grounded. What they like the most is to be needed and loved by their family. Everything else simply doesn't matter.

You can develop their loyalty if you give them praise and approval and are optimistic. Don't give them too much to do initially, and help them make decisions. They don't like to be hurried and will melt away if you are rude, harsh, or critical. They will only feel good about themselves if you make them feel good about themselves.

Lastly, when you ask them to do something, take the time to look into their eyes, speak softly with some kind words, don't complain, and tune in to what they are feeling. Remember that even though you may want them to do something for you, don't make it about you. Let them think you are helping them do something for them. When they know you are completely, 100 percent on their side, they will be there for you 110 percent—with bells on!

Prioritizing-Style Parent + Maintaining-Style Child

> We destroy the love of learning in children, which is so strong when they are small, by encouraging and compelling them to work for petty and contemptible rewards, gold stars, or papers marked 100 and tacked to the wall, or A's on report cards, or honor rolls, or dean's lists, or Phi Beta Kappa keys, in short, for the ignoble satisfaction of feeling that they are better than someone else.
>
> —John Holt, *randomterrain.com*

When the two of you work together, you can conquer the world—or at least the clutter in the bedroom. Prioritizing parents have the big picture in mind while your Maintainer child has the tenacity and organizing skills to take care of the details and make life a lot easier for you. While you come up with another big project to manage, they'll stick to the tasks at hand, no matter how difficult and time-consuming. It's a great setup. You take charge of the to-do's, and they take charge of the how-to-do's. Perfect!

They like existing structure and are not that big on changing things around, if they can help it. To teach them something new, it is best if you sound grounded, not illogical, and have a beginning, middle, and end to your line of thinking. They need reason to learn and are more methodical thinkers than you would imagine. They work much more slowly and tend not to make irrational decisions. Being very pragmatic, they don't want or have any desire to depart from what has been done in the past.

If something isn't right, the Maintainer child will criticize you and not blow up your ego. If you show any disregard for their talents, like complaining about the big effort in all the details, or think that schedules are ridiculous, they won't be happy. They aren't that demanding on themselves like you are. All they want is your approval and recognition for what they do. You must take the lead, as they are challenged with a crisis and the new and unexpected. They will not be happy if you contradict them and make them feel like their talents and gifts are a big waste of time. Let them take notes when you talk, or let them work slowly enough so they feel competent at what they are doing.

Maintainer kids are not big sharers and would rather work in private, with their own things all around them. They prefer not to be interrupted, and if you tell them what to do with a good, healthy approach, they will get right to work on it, by themselves. Team spirit doesn't really work for them, as they need to have time alone to process all the facts and figures in a way that looks right and works for them. It is to your benefit to leave them alone and only bother them if it is really necessary.

If you are very clear with what you want and need them to do, you can have a great relationship. They provide you with stability to flourish. You give them security. They are there to support you and do value time and giving you what you asked for. Don't exaggerate things and big future plans, as they care more about quality rather than speed. Don't demand that they skip steps. They are perfectionists and want to stay on track with what has been done before. They basically want to do it right rather than quickly or successfully.

Lastly, the Prioritizer parents have so many natural strengths. You are great leaders who can accomplish anything. You love the excitement and results of a grand conquest, and your decisive nature and ability to speak with authority cuts through other people's indecisiveness. You like to see the fruits of your labor A.S.A.P. And when you ask your children to do something, you demand it get done.

You tend to be impatient and short-tempered and may even be a bit autocratic if things aren't working out the way you like. Being more positive and sensitive to the needs of your family members is something new to conquer. Don't get hung up on their tendency to be slower than you. Maybe you can learn to schedule in some downtime to take five instead of checking another thing off the list.

Typologies are not about pigeonholing a child; they are dynamic living ways of understanding behavior. When you know your style or orientation, you automatically find comfort, strength, and then the ability to grow and change. All parents want to make their children's lives perfect. Please remember, be flexible.

Nothing will ever be perfect. As Judith Warner, author of *Perfect Madness,* says so well, "Women (and I'll add men) want to control their surroundings and create a perfect world for their children." Great intentions, but at what cost? Ellen Galinsky, in her book *Ask the Children,* claims that working mothers spend about eighteen minutes or even less on themselves each day. How can we push perfection when we don't have time to breathe?

The solution is to keep everything as simple as possible. Begin by setting aside one day during the school week on which no one has any extracurricular activities, or limit the number of lessons your kids take per week. Create more time! What makes children feel special and loved is the time they spend alone with you! Time creates room to explore, discover, and connect. As Mihaly Csikszentmihalyi claims in his book *Flow,* "When the activity enlivens your talents and skill, flow is apt to occur. We function the best when we are in flow."

CLOSING THOUGHTS

> Genuine success is more likely to occur when
> we know who we are innately and match the
> majority of our life's activities with what our
> brains do easily.
> —Arlene Taylor, *www.arlenetaylor.org*

As a professional organizer working with many families across the country, I can tell you that the number-one challenge in keeping our homes and lives in order, in an ever more complex world, is this: our belongings are taking over our space and our lives. This goes for ourselves and our children. Kids have too much stuff! I sometimes feel like I am drowning in a sea of crayons, CDs, hair accessories, notebook paper, stuffed animals, and batteries. I'll never forget walking into a beautiful home in Laguna Beach, California, to help a talented interior designer get organized. I decided to begin with her ten-year-old daughter's bedroom. I navigated my way to her dresser, pried opened the top three drawers, and out poured dozens upon dozens of bathing suits. I was knee-deep in nylon! Of course I wasn't surprised when I got to her mother's closet, also brimming with scarves, sunhats, and every kind of beach sandal!

Remember, the apple doesn't fall far from the tree. The more materialistic parents are, the more materialistic their children. Children model their parents, and so the good news is that you can affect and change them by changing yourself. As William Bennett says in *The Educated Child,* "You are your child's most important teacher." Because today's child grows up in a house that contains 50 percent more things than only twenty years ago, it is crucial that you create some limits. Children want to be around you, and they learn so much about life by just how you are. Face it: your children may not notice what you wear, but they certainly will notice your behavior. Take a stand and just say "No!" to endless consuming.

Kids, just like their parents, also overly identify with name-brand products. They often become obsessed with having to have the next Hello Kitty trinket or American Doll in the endless collection manufacturers churn out. Studies show that kids who are constant consumers are less happy and more frustrated on a daily basis. This kind of buying frenzy feeds on itself, building more wants, more things, more clutter, and more confusion. As Dan Kindlon says in *Too Much of a Good Thing,* "If we spoil our children with material goods in order to get a hug, or fail to set appropriate limits out of fear that they will withdraw their love, we have burdened them with protecting us from unhappiness." And as Edward, the Duke of Windsor, once said, "The thing that impresses me most about America is the way parents obey their children." Yes, parents run in circles to buy the next best thing, but ironically, 69 percent of kids say they'd rather hang out and spend time with their parents, compared with 13 percent who wish their parents would spend more money on them.

According to Juliet Schor, author of *Born to Shop,* in 2004, fifteen billion dollars were spent on advertising to woo children to want more and lure parents to spend more. Since the 1920s, toys have been marketed directly to children. Giving a couple simple toys to your child for Christmas now seems like a thing of the distant past. These days, parents spend the entire day reading manuals to figure out how to assemble the mile-high pile of gifts they've purchased to make sure their kids are "happy." Of course, the day after Christmas they realize their children have already tired of the booty, nor do they have the space to store all the new stuff! Do you spend your extra time loving your kids, or do you spend your extra time shopping for more? Remember, much of what we buy doesn't really improve our lives, but burdens and straps us down even more.

Thinking Style Provides a Roadmap

It's important to recognize that while you will never totally eliminate your kids' clutter, you *can* control it. By understanding your children's thinking style, giving them responsibilities appropriate for who they are, and making things easier for them to accomplish, you will make significant improvements in your closets, under the bed, and, most importantly, in your relationship with your children. Creating a structure that reflects their needs and passions will establish a more predictable and manageable life in which they can better succeed at home and at school. I'm really amazed at how ingenious kids are when it comes to problem-solving their own organizing woes. Give them room, some structured time, the right tools, and a couple tips just for them, and voilà! They are unstoppable!

Your child's brain, this three-pound remarkable universe, reflects his or her own unique temperament, desires, and preferences. It's obvious. Just observe something as simple as how a child tackles their homework. The Maintaining style might like to do their homework as soon as they get home from school. The Harmonizing style enjoys telling you about their day, being a part of dinner preparations, and chances are will like to do their homework around you. The Innovating style needs pushing and cajoling to crack that textbook. The Prioritizing style child lingers until right before bed and then settles down, pen in hand. Different strokes for different folks. As you learn to identify and then understand and respect your child's particular styles of thinking, your relationship will thrive, and so will they! You will discover how to communicate, motivate, and celebrate them exactly for who they are. Your children may not do it the way you do it, but over time, your frustration from imposing your style will disappear as you appreciate your child's talents and gifts. Remember, we are all works in progress, and as Maria Montessori demonstrated in her studies and classrooms, "A child readily obeys an adult. But when an adult asks him to renounce those instincts that favor his development, he cannot obey."

Teamwork is the way families can successfully work together to enjoy the fruits of each other's labor. In the *ITI*, which is a manual for Integrated Thematic Instruction, a teaching method that features brain-compatible learning, Susan Kovalik describes organization as, "To plan, arrange, and implement in an orderly way, to keep things orderly and ready to use." Kids want to do right. They want to please you. Guaranteed they will learn to pitch in, put things away, and take delight in having room to breathe. But you need to give your children opportunities to succeed. I assure you, they will! As H. Norman Wright encourages in *How to Talk So Your Kids Will Listen,* "The key to reducing your frustration over the child's quirks of behavior, and to communicate with him or her, is to understand and accommodate your child's unique personality style."

Routines, limits, structure, and discipline that reflect your child's unique thinking style aren't punitive, but rather, are life skills that will help them succeed in every way for the rest of their days. Eventually, these organizing skills become automatic. With repetition and awareness, connections are made between the neurons in the brain and skills are imprinted and solidified over time.

Start Small

In the beginning, organizing isn't always fun for kids. Seventy-five percent of the children out there need to *learn to* like it (though the Maintainers love it right off the bat!). Your challenge as a parent is to teach them how. When implementing your new-found insights into thinking style, don't try to demand too much right away. Focus on one thing they can easily change and improve. Have them practice it, master it, and then move on to the next. Even take before and after pictures so they can see what they accomplished. But don't forget to praise, praise, praise them for their accomplishments, large and small.

Beyond being able to walk into your child's room without tripping, the benefits of being organized are huge. Not only does it teach cooperation and responsibility, but also imbues a child with a deeper sense of competency, self-esteem, and independence. What a great way to really love and parent a child. As Mihaly Csikszentmihalyi, the author of *Flow* encourages us, "To experience such simple pleasures of parenting, one has to pay attention, to know what your child is proud of, what she is 'into', and then devote more attention to share those activities with her."

This is all about being present to what is and being authentic to it. When this happens, you are able to feel more connected and more kind. This entire exercise is really meant to make your life better, easier, more connected, and compassionate to different ways of thinking and, therefore, different ways of living. Everything we do is about making us happy. Having a better sense of what that is for you, by how you operate and having more of a sophisticated and conscious way to live life, will make you feel more confident, less threatened, and kinder.

This work is about creating a world where people are accepted and seen as being "a star" in their own life as they are able to understand and appreciate their uniqueness and be reminded by what they surround themselves with. You prosper when you feel well about yourself, positive, and good. And, therefore, you experience more of that when you become that. A deeper appreciation and connectedness to each other makes a world less intimidating and a lot more welcoming. Can you imagine a place where judgment doesn't exist and people feel free to roam in their own skin? Where people experience less discomfort and more interrelatedness within themselves and each other? This is what the big "O" in organizing is about—learning how to nurture someone's natural talents and then see them prosper, be happy, and have a positive influence in the world. As John F. Kennedy once said, "All of us do not have equal talent, but all of us should have an equal opportunity to develop our talent."

I wish you and your family good luck and lots of fun along the way.

BIBLIOGRAPHY

Education

Anderegg, David, Ph.D. *Worried All the Time.* New York: Free Press, 2003.

Armstrong, Thomas, Ph.D. *Awakening Your Child's Natural Genius.* New York: Jeremy P. Tarcher, 1991.

———. *In Their Own Way.* New York: Jeremy P. Tarcher, 2000.

———. *You're Smarter Than You Think.* Minneapolis: Free Spirit, 2003.

Aronson, Tara. *Mrs. Cleanjeans' Housekeeping with Kids.* New York: Rodale, 2004.

Baron-Cohen, Simon. *The Essential Difference: Men, Women and the Extreme Male Brain.* New York: Penguin, 2003.

Bartlett, John. *Bartlett's Familiar Quotations, Seventeenth Edition.* New York: Little, Brown and Company, 2002.

Bellamy, Rufus. *Inside the Brain.* North Mankato, MN: Smart Apple Media, 2005.

Bennett, William J., Chester E. Finn Jr., and John T. E. Cribb Jr. *The Educated Child.* New York: Free Press, 1999.

Britting, Jeff. *Ayn Rand.* New York: Overlook Duckworth, 2004.

Chandler, Christine, Ph.D., and Laura McGrath. *4 Weeks to a Better Behaved Child.* New York: McGraw-Hill, 2004.

Chin, Tiffani, Ph.D. *School Sense.* Santa Monica: Santa Monica Press, 2004.

Connelly, Megan. *The Smart Approach to Kids' Rooms.* New Jersey: Creative Homeowner, 2000.

Covey, Stephen. *The 7 Habits of Highly Effective Families.* New York: Golden Books, 1997.

Cox, Catharine Morris. *Early Mental Traits of Three Hundred Geniuses.* Stanford: Stanford University Press, 1926.

Crary, Elizabeth. *Pick Up Your Socks.* Seattle: Parenting Press, Inc., 1990.

———. *Without Spanking or Spoiling.* Seattle: Parenting Press, Inc., 1993.

Csikszentmihalyi, Mihaly. *Finding Flow.* New York: HarperCollins, 1997.

Davidson, Jay. *Teach Your Children Well.* Palo Alto, Tojabrel Press: 2001.

Declements, Barthe. *Spoiled Rotten.* New York: Hyperion Books, 1996.

Diamond, Marian, Ph.D., and Janet Hopson. *Magic Trees of the Mind.* New York: Dutton, 1998.

Dinkmeyer, Don Dr., and Dr. Gary D. McKay. *Raising a Responsible Child.* New York: Fireside, 1996.

Dosick, Wayne. *Golden Rules.* New York: HarperCollins, 1995.

Eagle, Dr. Carol J., and Carol Colman. *All That She Can Be.* New York: Simon & Schuster, 1993.

Eliot, Lise, Ph.D. *What's Going on in There?* New York: Bantam Books, 1999.

Elkind, David. *All Grown Up and No Place to Go.* New York: Addison-Wesley Publishing Company, 1984.

————. *The Hurried Child.* New York: Addison-Wesley Publishing Company, 1981.

Ellis, Elizabeth M., Ph.D. *Raising a Responsible Child.* New York: Birch Lane Press, 1995.

Fink, Jeff, and Jon Halpern. *Child Sense.* New Brighton: ChildSense, 2003.

Galinsky, Ellen. *Ask the Children.* New York: William Morrow and Company, Inc., 1999.

Glenn, H. Stephen, and Jane Nelsen. *Raising Self-Reliant Children in a Self-Indulgent World.* Rocklin: Prima Publishing and Communications, 1988.

Goethe, Johann Wolfgang von. *Hermann and Dorothea.* New York: Collier, 1961.

Goldman, Katherine Wyse. *My Mother Worked and I Turned Out Okay.* New York: Villard Books, 1993.

Gopnik, Alison, Ph.D., Andrew N. Meltzoff, Ph.D., and Patricia K. Kuhl, Ph.D. *Scientist in the Crib.* New York: William Morrow and Company, Inc., 1999.

Gordon, Dr. Thomas. *Discipline That Works.* New York: Plume Printing, 1991.

————. *Parent Effectiveness Training.* New York: David McKay Company, Inc., 1970.

————. *Teacher Effectiveness Training.* New York: David McKay Company, Inc., 1974.

Gurian, Michael. *The Good Son.* New York: Jeremy P. Tarcher/Putnam, 1999.

Hallowell, Edward M., M.D. *The Childhood Roots of Adult Happiness.* New York: Ballantine Books, 2002.

Hart, Leslie A. *Human Brain and Human Learning.* New York: Longman, 1983.

Healy, Jane M. *Failure to Connect.* New York: Simon & Schuster, 1998.

————. *Your Child's Growing Mind.* New York: Doubleday, 1994.

Henner, Marilu, and Ruth V. Sharon. *I Refuse to Raise a Brat.* New York: Regan Books, 1999.

Herrmann, Ned. *The Creative Brain.* Raleigh, NC: Ned Herrmann Group, 1989, 1993.

———. *The Whole Brain Business Book.* New York: McGraw-Hill, 1996.

Hirsh-Pasek, Kathy. *Einstein Never Used Flashcards.* New York: St. Martin's Press, 2003.

Howe, Neil. *Millennials Rising.* New York: Vintage Books, 2000.

Howe, Neil, and William Strauss. *The Next Generation.* New York: Vintage Books, 2000.

Ingersoll, Barbara D. *Distant Drums, Different Drummers.* Bethesda, MD: Cape Publications, Inc., 1995.

Isaacs, Susan, and Wendy Ritchey, Ph.D. *I Think I Can, I Know I Can.* New York: St. Martin's Press, 1989.

James, Elizabeth, and Carol Barkin. *How to Be School Smart.* New York: Lothrop, Lee and Shepard Books, 1998.

Kindlon, Dan, Ph.D. *Too Much of a Good Thing.* New York: Hyperion, 2001.

Klass, Perri, M.D., and Eileen Costello, M.D. *Quirky Kids.* New York: Ballantine Books, 2003.

Kovalik, Susan, and Karen Olsen. *ITI: The Model.* Kent: Books for Educators, Inc., 1994.

Kranowitz, Carol Stock. *The Out-of-Sync Child.* New York: Perigee, 1998

Krausse, Joachim, and Claude Lichtenstein. *Your Private Sky.* Baden: L. Muller, 1999.

Kurcinka, Mary Sheedy. *Raising Your Spirited Child.* New York: HarperCollins, 1992.

Levine, Mel, M.D. *A Mind at a Time.* New York: Simon & Schuster, 2002.

———. *Misunderstood Minds.* Boston: WGBH, 2002.

Lott, Lynn, and Riki Intner. *Chores Without Wars.* Rocklin: Prima Publishing, 1997.

———. *The Family That Works Together.* Rocklin: Prima Publishing, 1995.

MacKenzie, Robert, J. *Setting Limits.* Roseville: Prima Publishing, 1998.

Middleton, Haydn. *Ancient Greek Homes.* Chicago: Reed Educational and Professional Publishing, 2003.

Miller, Alice. *The Drama of the Gifted Child.* New York: Basic Books, 1997.

Mintz, Steven. *Huck's Raft.* Cambridge: Harvard University Press, 2004.

Moir, Anne, and David Jessel. *Brain Sex.* New York: Delta, 1989.

Montessori, Maria. *The Absorbent Mind.* New York: Henry Holt and Company, 1995.

————. *The Secret of Childhood.* New York: Ballantine Books, 1966.

Nelsen, Jane, and Lisa Larson. *Positive Discipline.* New York: Three Rivers Press, 2003.

Nelsen, Jane, Lisa Larson, and Roslyn Duffy. *Positive Discipline for Preschoolers.* Rocklin: Prima Publishing, 1995.

Newberger, Dr. Eli. *The Men They Will Become.* Cambridge: Perseus Publishing, 1999.

Olsen, Karen D., and Sue Pearson. *Character Begins at Home.* Kent: Susan Kovalik and Association, Inc., 2000.

Pearson, Sue. *Tools for Citizenship and Life.* Kent: Susan Kovalik and Association, Inc., 2000.

Perry, Susan K., Ph.D. *Playing Smart.* Minneapolis: Free Spirit Publishing, 2001.

Rapoport, Judith L., M.D. *The Boy Who Couldn't Stop Washing.* New York, E.P. Dutton, 1989.

Restak, Richard. *Mysteries of the Mind.* Washington, DC: National Geographic, 2000.

Reynolds, Eleanor. *Guiding Young Children.* Mountain View, CA: Mayfield Publishing Co., 1996.

Rogers, Lesley. *Sexing the Brain.* New York: Columbia University Press, 2001.

Rosenfeld, Alvin, M.D., and Nicole Wise. *Hyper-Parenting.* New York: St. Martin's Press, 2000.

Rousseau, Jean-Jacques. *Emile.* London: J.M. Dent, 1993.

Sax, Leonard. *Why Gender Matters.* New York: Doubleday, 2005.

Schor, Juliet B. *Born to Shop.* New York: Scribner, 2004.

Seligman, Martin, E.P., Karen Reivich, Lisa Jaycox, and Jane Gillham. *The Optimistic Child.* New York: Houghton Mifflin Co., 1995.

Shaw, Dr. Robert. *The Epidemic.* New York: Regan Books, 2003.

Smith, Karen A., Ph.D., and Karen R. Gouze, Ph.D. *The Sensory-Sensitive Child.* New York: HarperCollins, 2004.

Steinberg, Laurence, Ph.D. *The 10 Basic Principles of Good Parenting.* New York: Simon & Schuster, 2004.

Taylor Arlene. "The Brain Program Syllabus." Napa: self-published, 2003.

Twitchell, James B. *Branded Nation.* New York: Simon & Schuster, 2004.

Walsh, David, Ph.D. *Why Do They Act That Way?* New York: Free Press, 2004.

Warner, Judith. *Perfect Madness.* New York: Riverhead Books, 2005.

Wolfe, Patricia. *Brain Matters.* Alexandria: Association for Supervision and Curriculum Development, 2001.

Wright, H. Norman. *How to Talk So Your Kids Will Listen.* Ventura: Regal, 2004.

Children's Books on Organizing Themes

Baker, Alan. *Gray Rabbit's Odd One Out.* New York: Kingfisher, 1995.

Bourgeois, Paulette, and Brenda Clark. *Franklin Is Messy.* New York: Scholastic Inc., 1994.

Brett, Jan. *The Mitten.* New York: Scholastic, 1990.

Feiffer, Jules. *I Lost My Bear.* New York: Morrow Junior Books, 1998.

Glass, Julie, Dr., and Richard Walz. *The Fly on the Ceiling.* New York: Random House, 1998.

Hallowell, Edward M., M.D., and Bill Mayer. *A Walk in the Rain with a Brain.* New York: HarperCollins, 2004.

Hutchins, Pat. *Tidy Titch.* New York: Greenwillow Books, 1991.

James, Elizabeth, and Carol Barkin. *How to Be School Smart.* New York: Lothrop, Lee & Shepard Books, 1986.

Lindbergh, Anne, and Susan Hoguet. *Tidy Lady.* Orlando: Harcourt Brace Jovanovich, 1989.

McKenzie, Ellen Kindt, and Megan Lloyd. *The Perfectly Orderly House.* New York: Henry Holt and Co., Inc. 1994.

Menchin, Scott, and Ann Braybrooks. *Plenty of Pockets.* San Diego: Harcourt, Inc., 2000.

Milne, A. A. *Winnie the Pooh.* New York: E. P. Dutton, 1926.

Peters, Lisa, Westberg, and Brad Sneed. *When the Fly Flew In.* New York: Dial Books for Young Readers, 1994.

Peterson, Elise. *Tracy's Mess.* Boston: Whispering Coyote Press, Inc., 1996.

Teague, Mark. *Pigsty.* New York: Scholastic, Inc., 1994.

Testa, Fulvio. *Too Much Garbage.* New York: North-South Books, 2001.

Organization

Bykofsky, Sheree. *500 Terrific Ideas for Organizing Everything.* New York: Galahad Books, 1992.

Carter, Jarrett, Janae Carter, and Jolene Carter. *A Kid's Guide to Organizing.* Long Island, NY: Jehonadah Communications, 2002.

Davidson, Jay. *Teach Your Children Well.* Palo Alto: Tojabrel Press, 2001.

Kent, Cassandra. *Organizing Hints and Tips.* New York: DK Publishing, Inc., 1997.

Kyte, Kathy S. *In Charge.* New York: Alfred A. Knopf, 1983.

Linsenbach, Sherri. *The Everything Homeschooling Book.* Avon: Adams Media Corporation, 2003.

Manroe, Candace Ord. *Storage Made Easy.* Pleasantville: Reader's Digest, 1995.

Nelson, Mike. *Stop Clutter from Stealing Your Life.* Franklin Lakes, NJ: New Page Books, 2001.

Smallin, Donna. *Organizing Plain and Simple.* North Adams: Storey Publishing, 2002.

St. James, Elaine. *Simplify Your Life with Kids.* Kansas City: Andrews McMeel Publishing, 1997.

Vitale, Barbara Meister. *Unicorns Are Real.* Rolling Hills Estates, CA: Jalmar Press, 1982.

Other

Ebony. August 2004.

Ebony. January 2005.

Eyre, Denise. Interview, Saskatoon, Saskatchewan, December 2004.

Misunderstood Minds. Boston: WGBH Boston Video, 2002.

Newsweek, September 13, 2004.

U.S. News & World Report, "Mysteries of the Teen Years," May 2005.

Websites

www.allaboutmoms.com

www.amomslove.com

www.boston.com

www.brainyquote.com

www.capmag.com

www.cbc4kids.com

www.child.com

www.childfun.com

www.cyberparent.com

www.cyfernet.org

www.everydaytlc.com

www.fantasticstepmoms.com

www.gwu.edu

www.igrandparents.com

www.josephsoninstitute.com

www.MrMomZ.com

www.nationalgeographic.com

www.patwolfe.com

www.preschoolentertainment.com

www.randomterrain.com

www.rit.edu

www.selfgrowth.com

www.slowlane.com
www.stepcarefully.com
www.stepdads.com
www.stresslesscountry.com
www.teconline.com
www.wisdomquotes.com
www.zaadz.com
http://news.yahoo.com (12/9/2004)

Organized World®

To contact me for further information or to share with me stories about your children or students who exhibit these behaviors, I welcome any suggestions or comments at:

www.organizedworld.com
Lnakone@organizedworld.com

Lanna Nakone
Founder and president of
Organized World®
P O Box 457
Rutherford, CA 94573
707-524-9896
Fax: 707-963-1179

Available in 2007, Ms. Nakone's children's organizing product line will be available. Check out **www.organizedworld.com** for further information.

To contact:
Arlene Taylor, Ph.D.
www.arlenetaylor.org

To contact:
The National Association of Professional Organizers (NAPO)
4700 W. Lake Avenue
Glenview, IL 60025

USA Information   847-375-4746
USA Fax   877-734-8668
International/Canada Fax 732-578-2636
www.napo.net

INDEX

ABOUT THE AUTHOR

Alan Weissman

Internationally recognized professional organizer Lanna Nakone has been teaching people how to gain mastery over their physical environment for more than seven years. As the founder and driving force behind Organized World®, she has been featured in *Forbes, Cosmo, Self, Parenting,* and *Northbay Biz,* and a guest on CBC radio and CTV. A speaker for TEC, a company that educates CEOs around the world, she also instructs classes on residential organization at various colleges. Her client list includes BMW, Canyon Ranch, SBC Global, Harcourt-Brace, Mondavi Wineries, and Schramsberg Winery, among others.

Lanna's first book, *Organizing for Brain Type,* was released in 2005. Her column, "Lanna Nakone's Organized World," appears in *The Napa Valley Register.* Since 1999, Lanna has been a member of NAPO, the National Association of Professional Organizers, speaking annually at their National and Western Regional Conferences. She is currently developing a line of organizing products geared to brain style, which will be available in 2007.